Advertising Account Planning

New Strategies in the Digital Landscape

Carol J. Pardun
University of South Carolina

Beth E. Barnes
University of Kentucky

Sheri J. Broyles
University of North Texas

ROWMAN & LITTLEFIELD
Lanham • Boulder • New York • London

Executive Editor: Elizabeth Swayze
Assistant Editor: Megan Manzano
Senior Marketing Manager: Kim Lyons

Credits and acknowledgments for material borrowed from other sources, and
reproduced with permission, appear on the appropriate page within the text.

Published by Rowman & Littlefield
An imprint of The Rowman & Littlefield Publishing Group, Inc.
4501 Forbes Boulevard, Suite 200, Lanham, Maryland 20706
www.rowman.com

6 Tinworth Street, London SE11 5AL, United Kingdom

British Library Cataloguing in Publication Information Available

Library of Congress Cataloging-in-Publication Data
Names: Pardun, Carol J., author. | Barnes, Beth E., author. | Broyles, Sheri, author.
Title: Advertising account planning : new strategies in the digital landscape / Carol
    J. Pardun, University of South Carolina, Beth E. Barnes, University of Kentucky,
    Sheri Broyles, University of North Texas.
Description: Lanham : Rowman & Littlefield, [2020] | Includes bibliographical
    references and index.
Identifiers: LCCN 2019005089 (print) | LCCN 2019007374 (ebook) | ISBN
    9781538114087 (ebook) | ISBN 9781538114063 (cloth : alk. paper) | ISBN
    9781538114070 (pbk. : alk. paper)
Subjects: LCSH: Marketing research. | Advertising campaigns—Planning. |
    Advertising media planning. | Advertising—Management.
Classification: LCC HF5415.2 (ebook) | LCC HF5415.2 .P374 2020 (print) | DDC
    659.1/13—dc23
LC record available at https://lccn.loc.gov/2019005089

Contents

Preface

Thanks for reading *Advertising Account Planning: New Strategies in the Digital Landscape*. This book came about after I started teaching account planning on a regular basis. I wanted to focus on research tools and social media in a way that I hadn't seen covered in the few books that were available at the time. I asked two of my advertising friends to join me in the project—and they graciously jumped in! The book is much stronger with the contributions of Drs. Barnes and Broyles, and I thank them for joining me in thinking through how to create an account planning book that would connect with students.

Advertising Account Planning is organized around a typical university semester, covering a new topic roughly every week. At the end of each chapter we have included suggested activities that you can do in class (if your professor wants to) or that you can use on your own as a way to interact with the material.

After reading the book, I hope you'll see that advertising is not only complicated and changing rapidly but also a worthwhile endeavor, both as a potential career and as an academic subject worth studying.

Among my coauthors and myself, we have nearly a century of teaching experience. I'm guessing we have crossed paths with hundreds of advertising students over the years, yet we still get excited when a new semester is about to begin. Our students inspire us to continue thinking about advertising in new ways and to diligently figure out ways to better explain the advertising process to the next group of students who enter our classrooms. With that in mind, I'd like to thank all my recent advertising students at the University of South Carolina School of Journalism and Mass Communications. The future is bright for you all!

Carol J. Pardun
January 2019

CHAPTER 1

What Is Account Planning?

Walk into just about any advertising agency and you'll know you've entered a company that is vibrant and creative—and busy. If it's a large agency, you'll see all types of people. You've probably heard stories about indoor basketball hoops, late-night donut deliveries, and even a trampoline or two. While advertising agencies have myriad personalities (and some do, indeed, have indoor basketball courts!), certain categories of employees consistently exist within many agencies, regardless of their size.

If you know anything about the structure of an advertising agency, you know that lots of different jobs encompass what "people in advertising" do. The "creatives" develop the actual ads that we consume. This includes a bevy of copywriters, art directors, and graphic designers (and others, depending on the agency). And the "account" people do the work that helps the creatives succeed. These include media planners, media buyers, and account managers, just to name some of the main jobs. There are also account planners.

Ad Age published an article on September 15, 2003, that explained what account planning is. The writers defined account planning as "an approach for generating consumer insights that aid in the development of strategy and tactics and in evaluating communications campaigns." In other words, the account planner tries to deeply understand the consumer—and how to connect that knowledge of the consumer to the brand for which the advertising agency is responsible.

If you break down the *Ad Age* description, you'll see three main emphases for account planners: developing consumer insights, formulating a strategy for the advertising, and evaluating the effectiveness of the messaging. In its simplest forms, you can think of *consumer insights* as understanding the consumer in such a way that will help you connect the consumer and the brand. Developing an *advertising strategy* is similar to creating a map, pointing you in the right direction for a successful advertising campaign. And *evaluation* uses creative research tools to help you determine whether you're on the right path.

In other classes, you may have studied the basics of a SWOT analysis (strengths, weaknesses, opportunities, and threats). Using the SWOT framework is also helpful to think about what account planners do. As an account planner, you're helping the team figure out the *strengths and weaknesses of the brand* and the *opportunities and threats to the market of your brand.* Typically, this is accomplished using extensive secondary research (investigating as much as possible about what is already known about your brand and your potential target audience) and employing quantitative and qualitative primary research (original research that you do yourself) to further understand your target audience and your brand. This may also include studying trend reports and other insightful messaging that can help you project the opportunities and threats that may be awaiting the market in which your brand resides.

But ultimately the account planner has to commit to the following four core beliefs.

VOICE OF THE CONSUMER

Think of the account planner as the Voice of the Consumer. In the "ancient" media world (pre–social media) of a few broadcast television channels, thriving newspapers, and mainstream magazines, advertising agencies didn't have to worry about the consumer as much as they do in the present media environment. While it may be hard to imagine, limited media outlets typically resulted in a reduced need to understand the consumer beyond basic demographics because there were only a few media choices vying for your consumer's attention. In today's unlimited media landscape, however, it's imperative to deeply understand how a consumer thinks about the world. Media choices are now so segmented and so numerous that if you don't hit the right target audience, it's possible to lose contact with your consumer altogether.

It's no longer enough to only know the consumer's age, education, race, marital status, and such (typical demographics). It's not even enough to know the consumer's likes, attitudes, and beliefs (examples of psychographics). In today's media landscape, account planners also need to understand the consumer at such a level that they know beyond a doubt that the brand for which they are responsible will exactly fill the consumers' known (and unknown) needs and desires. If the account planners are responsible for a water brand, for example, they will need to know exactly why their consumers should drink Pellegrino and absolutely not Perrier. After all, the demographics and psychographics for both brands are remarkably similar. In fact, both brands are owned by the same company, Nestlé. Still, if you research these brands deeply enough, you'll discover that they attract a slightly different consumer. When either of these brands launches a new advertising campaign, the account planner needs to deeply understand these differences in order to match the right advertising approach to the consumers' heartfelt needs. And the account planner has to stand behind that understanding, explaining to everyone what the consumer is thinking, how the consumer will relate to the brand, and why the consumer wants this particular brand of water—and this kind only.

HEARTBEAT OF THE BRAND

Advocating on behalf of the consumer is one critical aspect of the account planner's job. However, that's just the beginning. Account planners also have to understand the inner workings, or heartbeat, of the brand itself—not just the features and benefits of the brand but also the deep-down "if this brand were a person, she would be my best friend" kind of knowledge.

Think about some of your favorite brands. Why do you like one brand better than the other? Sometimes it's obvious. Sometimes, one brand truly is better than the other. But often the product is similar or, in the case of a product such as a pain reliever, exactly the same. Or think about cola products. While Pepsi and Coca-Cola have spent untold millions over the years demonstrating differences between these two iconic brands, at the end of the day, these beverages are sugar, coloring, and water. Still, these are brands that command a loyalty other brands can only dream about. So why do you drink one cola brand but not the other? Great advertising captures the heart of the brand. And great account planners convey the heart of the brand to the creatives so copywriters and art directors can create the kind of advertising that connects with the right consumer.

PROTECTOR OF THE BRAND

While the account planners understand the consumer and the brand at levels few others in the agency might, they also need to protect the brand. They need to understand from where the brand originated, how it has grown (or decayed) over the years, and how it can move forward in a way that is consistent with the history of the brand. Rarely does an agency have the freedom to ignore whatever advertising has gone before and start from scratch. Account planners need to understand where the brand fits within the parent company, what its strengths and weaknesses are as well as the threats and opportunities that the market may face. (This is another reason using the SWOT analysis framework can be helpful.)

In order to protect the brand, account planners have to understand culture and trends. Account planners have to be able to read a graph, a research report, a Twitter comment, and someone's Instagram photo and be able to extrapolate how that might enhance or threaten the brand. Account planners need to know how to generate new thoughts from old information. And they must also know how to create new information with research methods such as surveys that will yield usable results. They must know how to conduct a focus group (or know how to hire a professional to do that). They must be able to know how to do some creative brainstorming exercises such as word associations and word mapping. Yet even with all these job requirements, account planners must do still more.

COMMUNICATOR TO THE CREATIVES

After account planners have investigated, analyzed, contemplated, and brainstormed, they have to be able to communicate these insights to the creative team. Account planners also have to feel such a connection to the consumer that they are able to accurately represent the consumer to the creative team.

Usually summarized in the creative brief (see chapter 13), the account planner has to be able to explain to the creatives the best approach for the advertising. The account planner will need to explain a lot of data quickly in a way that ensures the creative team understands the recommended approach. So, the account planner needs to have both strong presentation skills and writing prowess.

DO YOU HAVE WHAT IT TAKES TO BE AN ACCOUNT PLANNER?

How do you know if you have what it takes to be a successful account planner? The job description for an account planner is somewhat flexible depending on the size of the advertising agency and the department in which you'll be working. However, to be a successful account planner you should have these skills and interests:

Curiosity

When you're sitting at a coffee shop, sipping your favorite cup of morning ritual, do you watch other customers? What do you notice? Are you intrigued by those who boldly walk up to the counter and order a short dark decaf skinny macchiato? Or do you not even notice that there are others in the café? When you go to the grocery store, do you glance at the well-dressed businessman placing cereal in his basket? Do you wonder what he's having for dinner? While these questions might border on nosiness, from an account planner's perspective it's really about paying attention to everything around you—and finding *all of it incredibly interesting*. Everything is a story. Albert Einstein said this about curiosity: "The important thing is not to stop questioning. Curiosity has its own reason for existing." It's true. Curiosity leads to all sorts of insights. Curiosity is the first step to a successful account planning career.

Media Appreciation

Yes, media today suffer all sorts of challenges. But if you're an account planner, you need to be both a media consumer and someone who sees the benefits of a media-rich life. This means you need to appreciate all sorts of media—including advertising. If you see advertising as a mechanism to avoid at all costs (are you one of those who pays extra for Spotify to avoid the commercials, for example?), you need to think seriously about whether you're cut out for the world of advertising in general, and account planning in particular. Of course, you don't have to pay attention to every ad that comes your way, but your "advertising antenna" should always be at the ready. When good ads happen—whether on Facebook, on Spotify, or during the Super Bowl—do they grab your attention?

Creative Research Skills

As you'll see in later chapters, account planners are deeply involved in research. You'll need to develop and appreciate all sorts of data-gathering and analyzing abilities. But what sets the account planner apart from other researchers is the ability to use all the data points and make creative projections about what this means for the consumer and the brand. You need to appreciate quantitative data, of course, but the account planner needs to be able to look at data qualitatively as well and be willing to try all sorts of methods to arrive at unique consumer insights. It isn't just about summarizing data. It's about explaining what the data *mean*—and to use the data to better understand both the consumer and the brand.

Making Connections

Spotting trends is a skill that can be particularly beneficial to account planners. Account planners need to be able to know what is happening today, but they also need to make an educated guess about what will happen tomorrow. Spotting trends—but more important, predicting trends—can make an account planner invaluable to the brand. For example, the blog *Yogurt Lab* has published a food trend report for 2019. Among the trends the blog predicts are zero food waste, food recovery, and fermented foods. If your advertising agency recently acquired the brand Laughing Cow, for example, how could these trends help you better understand how to connect the consumer to your brand?

Voracious Reader

When was the last time you read a book that was not required for a class? If you don't immediately have an answer to that question, now is the time to make a change. Reading isn't just about gaining knowledge (although it can certainly help). Thomas Jefferson said, "I cannot live without books." We should all feel that way. Reading more than required classroom reading is not "wasted" time. It's a critical way to help you develop skills that are directly related to your ability to succeed as an account planner.

As a student interested in account planning, you need to be always thinking about things such as why people act the way they do, how people think about things, and what makes them happy. Reading keeps you on the forefront of this kind of thinking. J. J. Wong, cofounder of Creative Boost, wrote a blog piece in 2012 that explains eight reasons reading is important. Wong's list is as follows: (1) You expose yourself to new things; (2) Reading will lead to self-improvement; (3) Reading will improve your understanding of the world; (4) Reading will help you prepare to act; (5) You'll learn from others; (6) Reading will help your communication skills; (7) You'll improve your brain; and (8) Reading will improve your creativity.

Enthusiastic Writer

Do you love to write even if it is difficult for you? Do you enjoy the rhythm of words? After you've written something, do you review it and try to think of a way to make it better? If so, you'll enjoy being an account planner because you'll need to write a lot. From orchestrating the creative brief to writing trend reports, developing your writing skills will help you succeed. However, if you hate to write, think long and hard about whether you want to become an account planner.

An Appreciation for Neuroscience

While you don't have to be a brain scientist to be a successful account planner, significant progress has been made in recent years explaining why our brains act the way they do. Account planners should be learning as much as they can about the advances these scientists are making. A lot of the discoveries have direct importance to advertising effectiveness. It's remarkable how many books have been written by neuroscientists in language that the "regular" person can understand.

After reading this chapter, you may be excited about the world of account planning—or you may be completely intimidated about what it takes to be a good account planner. That's okay. This book will help you better understand what account planning is and how it fits into the larger world of advertising. We all hope at the very least that this book will inspire you to appreciate great advertising and consider the advertising field as a worthy career goal.

To get started, let's take a quick look at a successful account planner: Gerard Crichlow, strategy partner, Bacardi at AMV BBDO London. Here are some thoughts he has about account planning.

What made you want to become a planner/strategist?

I came in through the back door. I started my career in public relations working to influence reporters and the public that their products and services were important and worthy of getting on the front page of their publication of choice. But in PR you're often at the bottom of the marketing funnel, which means opportunities to shape the brand, its purpose, and how it behaves in the world is often dictated well before it ever came to us in PR. I wanted to be in a more creative environment and get more upstream in the decision-making process (e.g., what is the big idea, who should the brand partner with, what type of content should be made). I learned that strategic planners often had a seat at the table in shaping these decisions and were the voice of the consumer. You are what you do. So I started to think like a planner and, eventually, I became a planner.

What do you like most about planning/strategy development?

There are all types of strategists. Strategy is just a set of decisions that outline a plan of action. I love thinking through business problems, understanding a company, their target consumer, and deep-diving into the cultural context their brand is operating in. I also love collaborating with creatives to come up with creative solutions to real business issues. We have so many more canvases to play with that the opportunities to reach and entertain people is so varied it never gets dull.

What are the characteristics of a great strategist?

I've been fortunate to work with talented strategists in both the U.S. and the U.K., and while there are differences, great strategists have three things in common: (1) they are curious about the people, the world, technology, a niche subject; (2) they have a clear point of view on the world; and (3) they have empathy for the human condition.

Tapping into the human condition is essential to coming up with work that pulls at people's heartstrings or entertains their socks off. If you can't relate to them, you can't influence them.

Perhaps some thoughts about insights from focus groups or in-depth interviews with consumers?

This may be controversial, but I don't believe focus groups are the best ways to glean insights from real people. Nothing beats getting outside the office and talking with real people, observing their behaviors and asking direct questions. With social media, people are quick to share their opinions, and you can quickly tell if a message or piece of content is working or not. All we have to do is listen. As an industry we have to evolve how we do research and glean insights and more quickly put out content in the world.

SUGGESTED ACTIVITIES
TO HELP YOU THINK ABOUT THIS CHAPTER

Activity 1: In this chapter, you learned about three main emphases for account planners: developing consumer insights, formulating a strategy, and evaluating the effectiveness of the message. Now think about your interests. Which of these appeal to you? And why? Jot down notes that might be used in a class or group discussion.

Activity 2: An account planner is often considered the "consumer advocate." Pick a brand that you like and use—a brand that would be your "best friend." What three things does the consumer like most about the brand? Now take the other side. As the consumer advocate, what would the consumer like to see in the brand that isn't being talked about.

Activity 3: Do you have the skills and interests of an account planner? Circle the numbers that most reflect how you see yourself. Then total all the numbers. Where do you fall on the scale from 7 to 35? The lower the number, the more likely it is you might enjoy living in the world of an account planner.

I like "why questions."	1	2	3	4	5	I'm not very curious.
I like looking at ads.	1	2	3	4	5	I wish there weren't as many ads everywhere.
I enjoy learning new things.	1	2	3	4	5	I'm more comfortable around stuff I already know.
I like figuring out stuff.	1	2	3	4	5	I like it when I'm told what I should do.
I like to read just because.	1	2	3	4	5	I prefer other activities than reading.
I enjoy talking to strangers.	1	2	3	4	5	I prefer talking to people I know.
I enjoy writing.	1	2	3	4	5	Writing is one of my least favorite things.

REFERENCES

Wong, J. J. (n.d.). 8 reasons why reading is so important [Web log post]. *Inspiration Boost*. Retrieved from http://www.inspirationboost.com/8-reasons-why-reading-is-so-important

Yogurt Lab. (2018, February 14). 15 main food trends of 2019 [Web log post]. Retrieved from http://www.visityogurtlab.com/15-main-food-trends-2019.html

CHAPTER 2

Account Planning in the Age of Ad Clutter

P.S. It's All Ad Clutter

You sit down to watch your favorite binge TV show on Hulu only to hear "Due to streaming rights, a commercial will play at the start of your program." Or you open up your Facebook newsfeed to see an opportunity to buy a new skirt from Darn Good Yarn. Or perhaps when scrolling through your Twitter feed, you learn that Liberté yogurt wants you to try its new vanilla and cinnamon flavor.

It wasn't too long ago that one of the strongest advantages to TiVo (remember TiVo?) was that you could watch your favorite TV shows whenever you wanted to—all without advertising. It didn't take long before advertisers found creative ways to work around the TiVo environment. And while TiVo is still around, the playing field of "on-demand television" has expanded. Hulu, Netflix, Sling, and Amazon Prime are just a few examples of current popular on-demand options. Many of these on-demand programming options are still only a sliver of the consumer pie. For example, as of 2018, Sling had about 3 million subscribers compared to Netflix with 55 million and traditional cable subscribers at about 100 million. These new content formats demonstrate the ever-changing environment for relevant content. And these ever-expanding options not only complicate advertising strategies but also provide potential for more appropriately targeted branding messages.

As an account planner, this is good news for you. But it's also good news for you, the consumer. The reason is this: The more sophisticated the tools that allow consumers to choose the content they want to consume—and avoid the content that doesn't interest them—the more suitable the delivered advertising can be. Contrary to what some critics say, advertisers want to deliver ad content to the people who want to see it—that is, the potential target audience. After all, what's the point of showing advertising for fancy dog food to people who hate dogs? That is known as "advertising waste."

People often confuse advertising waste and advertising clutter. Both have negative connotations, but advertising "waste" is always undesirable while "clutter" in its best sense can be thought of as more opportunities to reach consumers. As the message targeting becomes more accurate, regardless of how much clutter exists, appropriately targeted consumers should actually be experiencing less "clutter" and more welcoming persuasive messaging.

The more advertisers understand what brands we want to connect with, the better they'll be able to match the appropriate advertising to our preferred media selections. The more appropriately targeted the advertising, the less advertisers have to spend on wasted eyeballs, and the more they can concentrate on delivering the kind of advertising that a consumer welcomes rather than tries to avoid.

Although eliminating all advertising waste might be the goal, unfortunately, it has yet to become a complete reality. So, welcome to the new world of ad clutter. We live in such a fast-paced media world it's still nearly impossible to target your message as accurately as you might want. In addition, there are so many choices available to advertisers and consumers alike it's difficult to completely understand a consumer's preferences. And with so many choices, it's difficult for consumers to "stay put" long enough for the advertisers to find them.

For example, do you prefer Spotify or Pandora? Or maybe Apple Music or SoundCloud? There is listener overlap between these platforms, of course, but there are also nuances that might make one platform more suitable to your target audience than another. Parker Hall of Digital Trends explains which people are better suited for a particular music platform. For example, he argues that Spotify is best for "new-musical explorers"; Pandora, for "passive" music listeners; and SoundCloud, for those who want to take a "hands-on approach to music discovery" (2019). As you can see, high-tech music delivery options, while sharing similarities, are not identical. Now scale this out to television, magazines, news sites, social media sites, and other media. It's easy to see why critics view the media landscape as a whole—and advertising in particular—as clutter.

But as account planners, it's time to think of "clutter" differently. Advertising delivery has fundamentally changed. The goal today should be to deliver only content that the consumers want to see (even if they don't know this yet). Improvements in technology have allowed this to be no longer a long-off dream but rather a real possibility. Technology continues to advance, and with that advancement, advertisers are able to improve content targeting. While it might sound cliché, it really is a win-win situation.

This shift has happened in part because of the migration from "interruption advertising" to "invitation advertising." Not too long ago, if advertisers wanted to get your attention, they simply bombarded you with messages until you finally gave up and paid attention. And then they bombarded you again. Advertisers understood that this method was inefficient, but it was the only option. The strategy was to advertise to enough people enough times to ensure that your message would ultimately get through to the right people. Unfortunately, this also meant that advertising was falling on some very annoyed ears and eyes. While less than ideal, advertisers thought the cost was worth it because there weren't a lot of other options—and if advertisers spent enough money placing ads in enough places, the advertising message would eventually reach the appropriate target audience.

James McQuivey of Forrester Research wrote about the end of advertising as we know it (2017). While he reported that Google made nearly $80 million in 2016 with interruption searches, he argues that interruption works only "if consumers spend time doing interruptible things on interruption-friendly devices." He argues that as technology and devices become sophisticated enough that consumers no longer need to be interrupted, they'll be less inclined to tolerate this kind of advertising. The forward-thinking account planner contemplates the future of advertising and works to deliver advertising strategies that will work well in this new advertising environment.

Because there are so many media choices today, advertisers can no longer afford to "throw the message out there," hoping it will hit the bull's-eye. Try as hard as they might, potential consumers are less likely to pay attention to your advertising if they aren't interested because they don't *have* to pay attention. They don't even have to notice because they can easily go to some other media platform. So, rather than interrupt your media experience, the smart advertiser "invites" you into the conversation in myriad ways. For example, perhaps you notice a sponsored post on your Facebook feed. It's for 12 Tomatoes, and they are offering a T-shirt that says, "That's what I do: I cook, and I know things." A handful of your Facebook friends "like" the page, and it doesn't surprise you. You like it as well. Your "foodie" friends find it amusing, and you're even thinking that maybe you'll buy one. So, you click on the link and consider buying the T-shirt.

If you buy the T-shirt and have a great experience in the process, the chance that you'll tell others about it is high. You have now "engaged" with the brand and have become an ambassador for it. If you think this is far-fetched, think about some of the particular brands that you're passionate about. You can probably think of at least one. Brand managers want to find more customers who are going to become involved (engaged) with the brand. Your job as an account planner, in part, is to help the brand manager identify those consumers.

This invitation, a highly engaged kind of advertising, isn't just for historically "low involvement" products like T-shirts or coffee. If the target audience and the product are matched well, a sponsored post on Facebook can attract a potential consumer who is in the market for an important "investment" product. For example, mattresses have recently entered the social media marketplace in a dramatic way. DreamCloud is a new "out of the box, direct to you" mattress company. Compared to buying a mattress at a bricks-and-mortar store, the DreamCloud is a bargain, but it's still over $1,000—far from an "I don't have to think about it" kind of project. Yet, DreamCloud advertises on Facebook, YouTube, and elsewhere in the social space. And the company has figured out ways to get consumers and potential consumers to "share" information about the product.

A picture of a luscious mattress shows up on your news feed inviting you to click for more information. Or not. Chances are if you're not in the market for a new mattress, you won't even see this sponsored post. And if you're not in the right economic strata, you won't see it either. But if you're in the market for a new mattress and the strategists have identified people like you as potentially good customers, finding the post on your Facebook page isn't a nuisance; it's a welcomed message—even if you didn't know this until you first saw the message. This is invitation advertising at its best.

Of course, in order for Facebook to provide this kind of advertising effectively, the company has to have access to our private information. Sure, we're all concerned about privacy these days (and that's a good thing), but it's important to remember that, ultimately, advertisers are really only interested in consumers who are in the right consumer community for their brands. The less content they provide that is ignored, the better. This isn't to say we should be lackadaisical with whom we choose to share our personal information. And with some serious platform breaches, ethical companies are working to be more open about the data they collect from us. But we should also remember that companies collect data *from* us to bring products that we want and need *to* us.

INTERNET OF THINGS

It's also important to understand that it isn't just advertisers who access this private information. We live in a culture that expects us to offer up all sorts of data about ourselves. And we do this willingly, if not eagerly, in order to get the kind of instant data access that makes our lives easier. Take IoT, for example. You can think of the "Internet of things" as basically any device (not including computers and your smartphone) that connects to the Internet. Fitness trackers, "smart" home thermostats, and Amazon's Alexa are all examples of IoT that we may have access to now. Andrew Meola wrote an article in *Business Insider* in May 2018 that says that by 2020, there will be 24 billion IoT devices in use. All this requires data (such as our current location for starters) that we're willing to hand over to the technology wizards in order to make our lives better.

NATIVE ADVERTISING

Native advertising is a logical step that advertisers have created that uses all that data to provide content that we want to see. Simply put, native advertising is online paid advertising that looks like nonadvertising content. In some ways, it's the ultimate example of "invitation advertising." It's important to understand, however, that not all digital advertising content is native advertising. For example, having a banner ad scroll across the top of a webpage that you're viewing isn't native advertising because it isn't a seamless addition to your nonadvertising content—neither is an ad that hijacks your YouTube video telling you that you can "skip the ad in four seconds." Those are examples of interruption advertising. Native ads require a seamless connection to your other data. Chances are you may not even be aware that the content is indeed paid (or "sponsored"), which leads some to argue that native advertising is deceptive.

To some critics, it's not just the potential deception of native advertising that is controversial. Some people find native ads manipulative, and even unethical, because viewers do not explicitly understand that they are seeing an ad. The problem is not just that the content "looks" like nonadvertising content but also, as critics have argued, that if it doesn't explicitly state that the content is "sponsored," it is inherently deceptive—and therefore unethical.

However, others have argued that perhaps advertising has evolved to the point that it's no longer necessary to identify itself as "advertising." Who cares where the content comes from as long as it's something we want to see? They argue that once we agree that "content is king," it doesn't matter where it comes from—especially if it's content we've been "invited" to see instead of content that has been pushed at us.

The growth of native advertising is exponential. Some argue that by 2021, nearly three-quarters of all advertising revenue will be some form of native. Some of the larger native advertising companies include Taboola, Outbrain, and Revcontent. There's even a Native Advertising Institute that offers lots of resources, research, and a yearly worldwide native advertising conference.

POEM

In marketing, the POEM model is widely discussed. But many researchers, marketers, advertisers, and professors haven't quite come to grasp with the implication of POEM for advertising strategy. POEM is an acronym for paid, owned, and earned media. Here's how to understand this from an advertising-creation perspective. *Paid* advertising is all the traditional advertising we're used to thinking about. Television commercials, full-page magazine ads, newspaper ads by the column inch, and radio morning-drive-time commercials are all examples of paid advertising. However, paid advertising also includes native ads, banner ads on websites, and Google AdWords, among others. The important thing to remember is that paid advertising alone is no longer enough to grab and hold the target audience's attention. Advertisers must use all their tools if they hope to engage their consumers in meaningful relationships. That brings us to the *owned* and *earned* options.

Owned media are controlled by the advertiser. An important example would be advertisers' YouTube channels. These could be channels that only offer versions of commercials that are seen on television (usually in a longer format), or they could be channels that offer all sorts of different content. The point is, the advertiser completely controls these channels and wants to create appropriate consumer communities that invite those interested in the message to take a look and stay awhile. A great example of owned media is the YouTube channel created by IKEA. IKEA runs ads showing its kitchen cabinets in magazines geared toward foodies (*Food Network Magazine*, for example). On its YouTube channel, it has long-form commercials showing families eating together in the kitchen with their cabinets in the background. In addition, it also hosts short "cooking shows" explaining how to make interesting dishes, all while showing IKEA kitchen cabinets.

Facebook can also be an example of owned media—if it's the Facebook page sponsored by the brand. The brand "runs" the page but often invites consumers to add content to the page.

With earned media, the consumer has the opportunity to weigh in, join the community, and perhaps even create some of the content that other potential consumers will see—and appreciate. All those "likes," retweets, and smiley faces that consumers use to express their feelings about a brand are forms of "earned" media.

When the POEM model of advertising is working at its best, the paid, owned, and earned messages all work together, creating a synergistic brand experience for the consumer. It's more than "integrated" communication. It's advertising that builds on the brand experience in an interactive—and inviting—way. Given the landscape of advertising clutter today, this is the only way advertising can thrive.

The Tide "It's a Tide Ad" campaign, showcased in the 2018 Super Bowl, is an example of the POEM model working at its best. In this campaign, Tide bought space for traditional length commercials, but it also bought several smaller ads, including some seven-seconds spots. The commercials featured "competitors" talking about their brands. (They used the actual brand if it was owned by Procter & Gamble. If not, they created made-up brands.) They were quickly interrupted, however, to be told that "It's a Tide Ad." In this way (and in good fun), Tide was able to "hijack" the entire football game as every commercial (and even the announcers) became a Tide commercial. It was all in good fun, but it was memorable. It generated an incredible amount of buzz and engagement as consumers used social media to post all sorts of photos with the hashtag "It'sATideAd."

Not only was no one offended by the Tide ad, but also they were intrigued by it. They shared their feelings about the campaign (and Tide), they created content, they looked at P&G's owned media, they watched the commercials, they tweeted their friends, and on and on. While some critics may have questioned the approach, both the ad community and the public embraced the concept. And the brand won all sorts of awards as a result, including the Cannes Lion Film Grand Prix, a top international award.

So while advertising is far from perfect, and we may all wish there wasn't so much of it around, as engagement advertising gets more sophisticated and reaches more people who are interested—and fewer people who are not—"ad clutter" may become less a concern in the future. At least that's what the astute account planner hopes for.

SUGGESTED ACTIVITIES
TO HELP YOU THINK ABOUT THIS CHAPTER

Activity 1: Do you prefer Spotify, Pandora, Apple Music, or SoundCloud? What is the personality of each of these brands? Why do you prefer your choice to the others?

Activity 2: The Internet of things (IoT) connects you to the Internet in many ways. It could be your fitness tracker, your refrigerator, or your thermostat. Make a list of all the things you currently own that are a part of IoT. Are you surprised? Why or why not?

Activity 3: Native advertising is online paid advertising that looks like nonadvertising content. Take a look at your favorite social media platform. How many native ads do you see? Does the content of these ads match your interests?

Activity 4: POEM is an acronym for paid, owned, and earned media. Give three examples of each of these in the media you use every day. Which do you think are the most effective? Why?

REFERENCES

Hall, Parker. (2019, January 22). The best music streaming services. Digital Trends. Retrieved from https://www.digitaltrends.com/music/best-music-streaming-services

McQuivey, J. (2017, May 15). The end of advertising as we know it. *Forbes*. Retrieved from https://www.forbes.com/sites/forrester/2017/05/15/the-end-of-advertising-as-we-know-it

Native Advertising Institute. (n.d.). Research. Retrieved from https://nativeadvertising institute.com/resources/research

CHAPTER 3

What Is a Brand?

Whether working in an agency or client-side setting, the brand is the foundation of the planner's thinking and efforts. As we said in chapter 1, two of the planner's primary responsibilities are to be the heartbeat and the protector of the brand. Protecting and championing the brand goes hand in hand with the responsibility of being the voice of the consumer in the advertising development process. Why? Because brands exist in the mind of the consumer.

The company and the agency certainly play major roles in defining the brand, and much of what we'll look at in this chapter comes from industry and consumer research that we hope will help you think about brands in ways you may not have done before. But in the end, the brand is what the consumer thinks it is. The strongest, best-performing brands have all achieved a level of consumer recognition and understanding that makes them very strong against both established and new competitors.

When it comes to brands and branding, one of the top names in the industry is Interbrand. A global branding consultancy with offices in 17 countries, Interbrand is focused on helping clients strengthen their brands. Interbrand also provides an important resource for planners, brandchannel (www.brandchannel.com), a one-stop shop for information on branding and current trends.

One of brandchannel's services is its branding glossary. So, let's start with a basic definition. What is a brand?

[A brand is] a living business asset, designed to enhance the connection between a business and customer or consumer. A brand is the way in which people understand, navigate and talk about a company's business strategy and it simplifies decision-making when selecting a product or service. A brand helps ensure relationships that secure and create future earnings by driving demand, commanding a premium and engendering loyalty. Once simply considered trademarks or logos/logotypes, brands deliver tangible economic value. (brandchannel, n.d.)

There's a lot going on in that definition. Let's look at some of the elements.

Enhancing the connection between a business and its customers or consumers is all about building and maintaining relationships. Brands are an important part of our lives. At a basic level, they're the things we put in and on our bodies, where we live, and how we get around. But they also communicate a great deal about us to other people, and they affect how we see ourselves as well. Finding the aspects of those connections that resonate the most deeply with consumers is a fundamental part of the planner's job.

Simplifying decision-making is an important benefit. While shopping can certainly be fun, in many cases it's more of a necessary chore for most of us. Brands provide a shortcut because they provide consistency over time in terms of quality, pricing, and performance relative to the alternatives. With established brands, you know what you're getting, and if the brand somehow doesn't deliver on what it has promised, there's usually a way to get your money back or some other type of redress. Social media have provided a means to let others know about brand experiences, both good and also, definitely, bad. Brands live and die on their reputations, and consistency is a huge factor. Most brands have an implicit message that the consumer should trust them to work as advertised.

The last part of brandchannel's definition deals with the economic and financial aspect of brands. While loyalty can be hard to earn and takes work to maintain over time, it's an important and valuable asset for a brand. Loyal customers are willing to pay more for a brand than for its competition. They're also resistant to sales promotion offers made by those competitors. The 80/20 rule holds that 80% of a brand's business will come from 20% (or fewer) of its customers. It's that highly loyal 20% group that a planner needs to always keep in mind.

BRAND KNOWLEDGE

As we mentioned at the outset, the brand belongs to the consumer as much as, if not more than, it does to the company behind the brand. A brand's image comes from what consumers consider it to be. The company and planner can do things to affect that image, but a brand is what the consumer thinks it is. So, one of the first jobs of the planner is to really think through the brand carefully, and to do so from the perspective of the consumer. We'll discuss some of the kinds of research that can be used to figure out consumer perceptions in later chapters, but for now, let's look at what elements go into this consumer-originated image.

Dr. Kevin Lane Keller of Dartmouth has done a significant amount of work looking at branding topics, including brand image. His brand knowledge model is shown in figure 3.1 (Keller, 1993). As you can see, Keller's model has two main components, brand awareness and brand image. Consumers have to first know of a brand in order to know anything about it. Brand awareness has dimensions of recall and recognition. Recall deals with whether the brand is one that is stored in the consumers' memory, a brand they've come into contact with in some way in the past. Recognition has to do with knowing what the brand is when hearing its name, seeing its package, or coming across an ad for the brand, or such experiences. Recall is generally seen as the stronger of the two, but recognition is what happens in shopping experiences. Brand goals related to awareness are a driving force behind many advertising decisions, especially media planning decisions.

The second component, brand image, is more complex. And it's a critically important area for a planner to explore. Brand image looks at the types of things the consumer associates with the brand, how favorable (or not) those associations are, how strong the associations are, and how unique they are. The associations can fall into three categories: attributes, benefits, and attitudes.

Attributes are things you'd use in describing a product or service. They can be directly product related, such as the size, flavor, shape, durability, and so on, or they can be non-product related, such as how much the brand costs, the packaging it comes in, the consumer's ideas about the kinds of

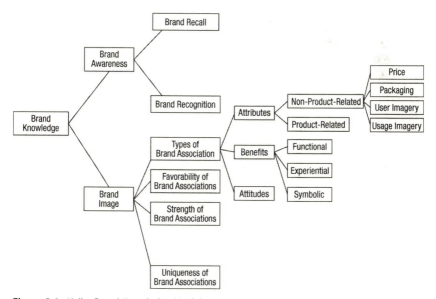

Figure 3.1. Keller Brand Knowledge Model

people who use that brand (user imagery), and when and where the brand is most appropriately used (usage imagery). Much of what gets focused on in advertising for a brand are these kinds of product-related and non-product-related attributes, and they play an important role in developing the image of the brand. Planners think about which attributes are most important to the target audience for the brand and which ones will be most powerful in setting the brand apart from its competitors and driving purchasing decisions. So, a planner really needs to know and understand the brand's attributes in as much detail as possible.

Benefits are how the attributes help the consumer. The brand's benefit is what it does or will do for the consumer, the core promise the brand makes. Determining what the benefits are coming out of the brand's attributes—and which benefit will be most important to consumers—is a critical part of the planner's job. What will people care most about? What does our brand perform best? Those benefits directly tied to product-related attributes are considered functional benefits, because they help describe the function of the brand. Experiential benefits are a second category having to do with what it's like to use the brand and how that usage situation feels. Symbolic benefits are a little more abstract and often come out of the non-product-related attributes. I might, for example, choose a high-priced product within a category because it will signify success, both to me and to others who see me using that brand.

Many brands offer multiple benefits, but effective advertising is all about keeping things simple and direct. Which benefit matters the most to the target audience? Which benefit is the most compelling aspect to build a creative brief, and a campaign, around that will drive sales?

Brand attitudes are just that, the consumer's attitude toward the brand. Is it viewed favorably? Or are attitudes toward the brand negative? Determining attitudes and, as important, the reasons underlying those attitudes, is another aspect of the planner's role. Figuring out the existing attitudes the consumers have toward the brand and what's underlying those attitudes can help in unlocking insights to focus on in the advertising campaign. We'll return to this in the next few chapters where we look at research methods.

The other parts of Keller's model build on the brand associations. We need to know how favorable all the associations are, both for the brand itself and with regard to competitive brands. The strength of the associations has to do with both how much the consumer knows about the brand and where that knowledge comes from—that is, the quality of the information. Knowledge based on personal use is stronger than that based on brand communication claims alone. For example, knowledge from trusted friends is stronger than that from impersonal media sources. Finally, the uniqueness of the associations concerns how different the consumer's associations with this brand are from what they know and think about other brands. As we'll see in the next section, the uniqueness aspect is one of the fundamentals when it comes to building a strong brand.

While others have also studied and written about brand knowledge, Keller's model lays out the key elements plainly. You might not put a copy of the model up in your office, or bookmark it on your smartphone, but it's not a bad idea. When you find yourself struggling for an idea as you're developing a brief, we recommend using this model as a touchpoint to bring your thinking back to the brand.

BRANDING MODELS

Once you have a handle on what your brand currently means to consumers, you can start to think about ways to strengthen the brand. That might mean reinforcing an existing positive image or trying to change a negative image. Because building and nurturing strong brands is so essential to business success (and an important aspect of the planner's job), there are a number of branding models and brand evaluation tools available. The various models differ in complexity and detail, and as your career develops, you might even come up with your own. To start you off, we'll look at two approaches, one very basic and the other a bit more complex. Both, though, offer good ways to explore a brand in more detail and think about what aspects of the brand might be the basis for a terrific advertising campaign.

Y&R Brand Asset Valuator

One of the most basic branding models is the Brand Asset Valuator developed by the Young & Rubicam agency (https://www.yr.com/bav). The Brand Asset Valuator has fewer elements than many other models (its simplicity is part of its strength), making it relatively easy to apply, even if you're not a branding expert.

The Brand Asset Valuator looks at brands on two dimensions, Brand Strength and Brand Stature. Each of those elements is further subdivided into two components. Brand Strength is made up of Differentiation and Relevance, while Brand Stature focuses on Esteem and Knowledge. Brand Strength looks at how well poised the brand is for growth in the future, while Brand Stature is about current performance (see figure 3.2).

Here's how Y&R talks about each of the four elements:

Differentiation: "A brand's ability to capture attention in the cultural landscape. A powerful driver of curiosity, advocacy and pricing power."
Relevance: "How appropriate and meaningful a brand is to consumers. Drives brand consideration and trial."

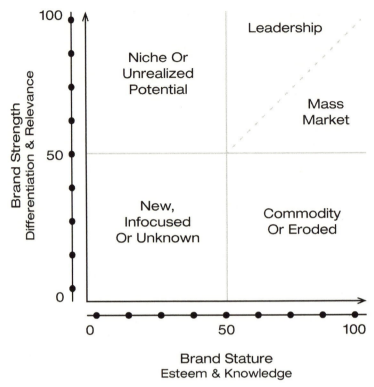

Figure 3.2. Y&R BAV Grid. *Source*: BAV Group. (n.d.). BrandAsset Valuator. Retrieved from https://www.bavgroup.com/about-bav/brandassetr-valuator

Esteem: "A measure of how highly regarded a brand is and how well it delivers on its promises. Leads to trial and commitment."

Knowledge: "The depth of understanding people have of a brand—both its positive and negative information." (BAV Group, n.d.)

These four elements, or pillars in Y&R's terminology, are essential elements of a brand and things a planner needs to think about in developing brand communication materials, especially advertising. Differentiation is the first and, in many ways, the most important aspect. Put simply, if there isn't something that sets your brand apart from its competitors, you don't really have a brand, or at least not a strong brand. If you're lucky, the differentiation will be an integral part of the product or service itself, something it has or does that no competitor has. For example, many aspects of Apple's technology products are unique to that brand, including its operating system and many of its design elements. In many cases, though, there may not be real, physical differentiation. In that situation, part of the planner's job may be to help develop a differentiation strategy that deals with psychological differentiation, creating difference through how the brand is talked about and promoted. An example would be Coca-Cola. As we mentioned earlier, its physical products aren't tremendously different than those of its competitors, but it has created a powerful, differentiated image over time.

While Relevance is rooted in the product or service itself and the main benefit it provides, it also has a lot to do with carefully evaluating the possible target audience. Who most needs or would most want that benefit? Where do we need to talk about the brand, and what do we need to say about it to help that group of people see its relevance to them? Because part of the planner's responsibility is being the voice of the consumer within the agency, relevance is a critical consideration.

Esteem comes at least in part from the values the brand stands for and how well it delivers on the promise it makes to consumers. We'll look at some of the research tools planners can use to identify values in chapter 9. For now, know that the planner needs to have a clear idea of what the brand, and the company behind the brand, stand for so that those values become part of all brand communications.

When you first get a brand assignment to work on, start by jotting down your initial thoughts in each of the four areas of differentiation, relevance, esteem, and knowledge. If you have trouble characterizing the brand in any of those areas, that's an indication of where work needs to be done. It can be a good starting point for developing your campaign, or at least for suggesting which areas you need to look at most closely when you start your research.

Interbrand Best Brands

While we like the Y&R Brand Asset Valuator for its simplicity and focus, it's important to know that there are other, more complex branding models that are also widely used. For example, each year, Interbrand releases its Best Brands list, a ranking of the Top 100 global brands based on Interbrand's valuation of those brands (Interbrand, n.d.). The brand valuation model has three components: (1) financial analysis, which looks at how profitable the brand is; (2) role of brand, an estimate of how important the brand alone is to the consumer's purchase decision (i.e., how much would someone pay for the exact same product if it didn't have that brand's name on it?); and (3) brand strength, which incorporates 10 factors that are evaluated in comparison to other brands. The financial analysis and role of brand elements are both essential, but we'll focus on the 10 factors of brand strength. They include a number of considerations for strategists, more aspects of the brand that need exploration and that might be the basis for a winning ad campaign.

Interbrand classifies the first four factors as internal dimensions—the things the company behind the brand needs to do (and keep doing over time) to keep the brand strong. Those include (1) clarity, or what the brand stands for; (2) commitment, the kind and degree of support the brand receives from the organization; (3) governance, how the company is run and makes decisions; and (4) responsiveness, how agile the company is at monitoring and reacting to change. A planner may not be able to directly affect the four internal dimensions, but these dimensions will certainly have an effect on the planner's ability to support the brand.

The other six factors are external dimensions. Brand promotion, including advertising, plays an important role in determining and communicating these dimensions to both current and prospective customers, so the planner needs to be focused on these attributes:

- *Authenticity.* This is the brand's story, where it comes from, what it stands for. It's where the brand's values come in. It's not an accident that more and more brands are telling their origin stories; consumers care about what brands stand for and how they came to be.
- *Consistency.* Not just how the brand performs over time or from purchase to purchase, but also how consistent the brand's messages are within and across communication platforms. Am I telling you that I'm the highest-quality brand in the category in my advertising but at the same time offering deep discounts in my sales promotion efforts? That's not being consistent and sends mixed messages to your audience.
- *Differentiation.* We talked about this with the Brand Asset Valuator. It's difficult to imagine a useful branding model that doesn't include differentiation. Your brand *must* be seen as offering something different than the alternatives.
- *Engagement.* How well consumers understand the brand and the strength of the relationship they have with it. A lot of attention is given to how to engage consumers with brands, so it's something planners deal with on an ongoing basis. Engagement is tied directly to emotion and consumers' emotional attachment to the brand, something we'll explore in more detail shortly.
- *Presence.* How well known is the brand? How and where and how often is it talked about? Presence is another way of thinking about the brand awareness aspect of the Keller model.
- *Relevance.* Another element we looked at earlier. Where does the brand fit into the consumer's life? How good is that fit? (Interbrand, n.d.)

The top 10 brands from the 2018 Top Global Brands are listed in table 3.1; you can see the full list at https://www.interbrand.com/best-brands/

Table 3.1. Interbrand Top 10 Global Brands, 2018

Rank	Brand	Brand Value Growth	Brand Value
1	Apple	+16%	$214,480,000
2	Google	+10%	$155,506,000
3	Amazon	+56%	$100,764,000
4	Microsoft	+16%	$92,715,000
5	Coca-Cola	−5%	$66,341,000
6	Samsung	+6%	$59,890,000
7	Toyota	+6%	$53,404,000
8	Mercedes-Benz	+2%	$48,601,000
9	Facebook	−6%	$45,168,000
10	McDonald's	+5%	$43,417,000

best-global-brands/2018/. The table lists the brand's ranking, name, its growth in brand value (that unique contribution of the brand to purchasing decisions) since 2017, and the dollar amount of the brand's value. Chances are you'll recognize most, if not all, of the brands listed here and in the full listing of the top 100. After all, they're on the list because they're strong brands.

If you spend time on the Interbrand Best Brands website, you can read more about the thinking behind Best Brands and exactly how the evaluation is done, as well as keep up with the new listings each year. There are also numerous reports looking at brands in specific countries and key world regions. As you work on developing your planning skills, it's worth taking some time to find out what the strongest brands are, and to think about what makes them strong, particularly in terms of their advertising approach and the way consumers see them compared to their competitors. What makes a great brand great?

BRAND LOVE

As you'll recall, engagement is one of the elements of Interbrand's branding model. Consumers engage with brands they care about. A brand's loyal, connected group of customers oftentimes doesn't just really like a particular brand; they love it. The concept of loving a brand is something that both the advertising industry and academic researchers in this field have spent a lot of time looking at and thinking about. As more of the work coming out of bioscience has shown the crucial importance of emotion in all decision-making, including decisions that on the surface seem strictly rational, the importance of an emotional tie between a brand and its customers has become more obvious, and something that planners work to nurture. How can you help your brand become loved?

Saatchi & Saatchi's Lovemarks

While every advertising agency spends time thinking about the emotional connections between consumers and the brands the agency represents, Saatchi & Saatchi is probably the agency most closely associated with the idea of the primacy of emotion. They call their approach "Lovemarks," and as you might guess, it's all about those emotional ties. According to Saatchi & Saatchi, "Lovemarks reach your heart as well as your mind, creating an intimate, emotional connection that you just can't live without. Ever. . . . Put simply, Lovemarks inspire: Loyalty Beyond Reason" (Lovemarks, n.d.).

As figure 3.3 shows, in Saatchi & Saatchi's conception, Lovemarks happen when brands are high both on respect and on love. Respect is self-explanatory, and it relates to that idea of consistency and trust mentioned previously. What about love? Lovemarks' love has three elements: mystery, sensuality, and intimacy. (We're definitely talking high emotions here.) Mystery has to do with the brand's story and how effectively it's communicated.

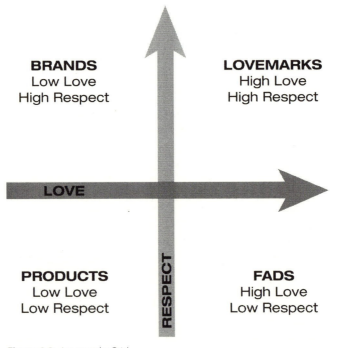

BRANDS
Low Love
High Respect

LOVEMARKS
High Love
High Respect

LOVE

PRODUCTS
Low Love
Low Respect

RESPECT

FADS
High Love
Low Respect

Figure 3.3. Lovemarks Grid

Sensuality looks at how the brand performs with regard to our five senses of taste, touch, smell, sound, and sight. Intimacy is about the connection between the brand and its customer, particularly the depth of that connection (Lovemarks, n.d.).

You can learn much more about Lovemarks, including how to apply Lovemarks' thinking to brand building, at Lovemarks Campus (http://www .lovemarkscampus.com). This site has a number of resources designed for both students and practitioners, including information on Saatchi & Saatchi's Lovemap software. (See chapter 6 for more on Lovemarks Campus.)

How does the Lovemarks mind-set work in practice? Saatchi & Saatchi's client list includes 6 of the top 10 global advertisers (Saatchi & Saatchi, n.d.b). Some of the brands they help to nurture are Tide laundry detergent, Walmart, Olay beauty care, USAA insurance, Pampers and Luvs diapers, and Head & Shoulders hair care (Saatchi & Saatchi New York, n.d.). And those are just a few of the brands tied to Saatchi & Saatchi's New York office. As a global firm, Saatchi & Saatchi operates in 67 countries (Saatchi & Saatchi, n.d.a).

To look at just one of those brands as an example, USAA enjoys intense devotion from its customers. You may have seen some of their ads where customers talk about their positive interactions with the company. Most of the ads end with the customers stating their name and then saying, "And I'm a USAA member for life." That's not just ad talk; according to USAA's fact sheet posted on their website, the company's customer retention rate in 2017 was 98%. While it can be a hassle to change insurance companies, the average retention rate in the insurance industry is only about 84%, so USAA is really outperforming the industry. USAA customers don't just like their insurance company; they love it.

On the academic side, brand experts Drs. Rajeev Batra, Aaron Ahuvia, and Richard P. Bagozzi sought to define the components of brand love. Their article, "Brand Love," was published in the *Journal of Marketing* in 2012. As one of the most prominent mainstream academic journals in the marketing field, the *Journal of Marketing*'s endorsement of the research sent a clear signal of the importance of emotion at the center of brand building.

Batra, Ahuvia, and Bagozzi (2012) argued that while many researchers in both the industry and the academy were talking about consumers' love for particular brands, no one had clearly defined what brand love entailed. Based on interviews with a number of consumers, they conceptualized brand love as a multifaceted construct, and by listening to how consumers talked about the brands they loved, they were able to identify seven components of brand love, as shown in figure 3.4. (With brands, as with people, love is complicated!)

Let's look at each of the seven components to better understand the emotional connection that can develop between consumers and much-loved

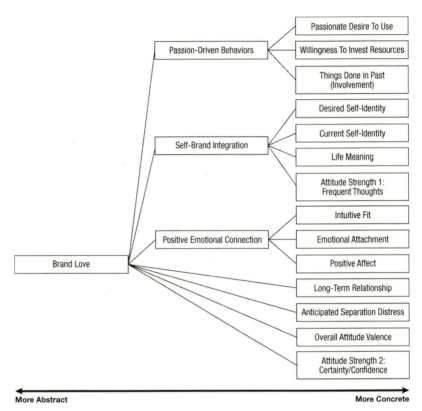

Figure 3.4. Brand Love Model. *Source:* Batra, R., Ahuvia, A., Bagozzi, R. P. (2012, March). Brand love. *Journal of Marketing, 76,* 10.

brands. As you read through the components, it may help to have a brand in mind that you yourself love, or a brand you're working with currently.

1. *Passion-driven behaviors.* When we really love a brand, we're willing to spend time and money with that brand, and we really enjoy and look forward to using that brand. We also usually have a history with the brand. It's one we've used over time and come back to again and again.
2. *Self-brand integration.* This is about how using the brand makes us feel about ourselves, both the person we are now and the person we aspire to be. Loved brands are affirming and are often seen as things that are helping us to improve who we are. We think about those brands a lot, and they help to give meaning to our lives, or at least to the aspect of our lives that they are part of.

3. *Positive emotional connection.* With brands, as often with people, loving begins in liking. We love brands that we have a positive attitude toward, that feel as if they fit us.

4. *Long-term relationship.* People speak of loved brands in terms of commitment. Most brands we love are brands we've used often and that we hope to be able to continue to use into the future. Recall USAA's "member for life" message.

5. *Anticipated separation distress.* As noted above, we want to keep using a loved brand. Anticipated separation distress is the degree to which we'd miss a brand and feel lost if it went away.

6. *Overall attitude valence.* This element deals with our feelings on how well the brand meets our needs and how it compares to both other brands and our idea of the ideal brand in that category.

7. *Attitude certainty/confidence.* This final element concerns how confident we are that our feelings for and perceptions of the brand are accurate and will hold up over time.

How can knowing the existence and importance of brand love help a planner in developing ideas for promoting a brand? One consideration is how to make the brand lovable. Can the brand be personalized or customized to make it more appealing? (Coca-Cola's "Share a Coke" campaign with its personalized bottles is a great example.) How about finding ways to increase consumers' interactions with the brand, such as through a branded app or a loyalty program that encourages frequent use? (The thinking here is the better you know a brand, the more likely it is you'll come to love that brand.)

Loyalty programs have become popular among brand marketers for just this reason. A 2017 study looked at more than 400 different loyalty programs and found that the typical U.S. consumer belonged to 14.3 programs. However, that same typical consumer was only active in about half of the programs they belonged to. Clearly loyalty can't be taken for granted just because your brand has a loyalty program. What people want are programs that are personalized, are easy to use, and truly make them feel special (Bond Brand Loyalty, 2017).

The planner might also develop ideas to build emotional connections as well as strengthen positive attitudes. Increasingly, and particularly with Millennial consumers, studies are showing that people actually care about the company behind the brand and the values that company upholds (Edelman, 2017). It's that authenticity idea from the Interbrand model. For some brands, a lot of the love they get from consumers comes as much from the company's activities regarding corporate social responsibility (CSR) as from the product itself. Think of TOMS Shoes, for example, and its pledge to donate items to people in need in more than 70 countries. Each purchase made from TOMS sparks a donation, with the particulars tied to the product purchased (TOMS, n.d.).

The positive attitudes that can flow from a strong CSR focus can even help to create a brand from scratch. Lokono is a company that sells backpacks made by women in the mountains of Nicaragua using fabric they weave using material from recycled clothing. Proceeds from the sale of the backpacks are used to buy school supplies for children in Nicaragua. The company was created by two guys from the United States who had done volunteer teaching in Nicaragua after graduating from college. They saw that, although schooling is free in the country, kids have to provide their own supplies. Many aren't able to do so and so stop going to school. With Lokono, a social need existed before the product idea and brand were ever developed (Lokono, n.d.).

Another possible way for a strategist to build love for a brand, particularly if it's in a product category that's often taken for granted, is to develop ideas to get people to think about how they would feel if that brand were gone. McDonald's has done this for years with its McRib sandwich, only making it available for a limited time. Disney does the same with many of its movie releases, only making them available for home purchase on DVD or Blu-ray for a limited period of time before they go into the Disney Vault (Taylor, 2017).

By now, you can see the power that love holds for brands as well as for people. Just as we encouraged you to look at and think carefully about the brands on Interbrand's Best Brands list, it's worth your time to explore the thinking and messages behind brands that are loved. What are some of the best-loved brands? That's something that another branding consultancy works to identify.

Brand Keys Customer Loyalty Engagement Index

Brand Keys, a branding consultancy with offices in seven countries, focuses on helping its clients understand and build consumer loyalty to their brands. Each year, Brand Keys publishes its Customer Loyalty Engagement Index. Put simply, the index identifies the brand in a wide range of product categories (84 in 2018) that does the best job of meeting or exceeding consumer expectations. Brand Keys does this by first identifying the key factors, or drivers, that affect decision-making for the product category, and then evaluates how close individual brands are to the category ideal (Brand Keys, n.d.). While the Customer Loyalty Engagement Index isn't specifically a list of loved brands, it's a pretty good indication of which brands are doing the best job of tapping into what consumers want and value. A list of the category leaders in a number of product categories is shown

Table 3.2.   Customer Loyalty Engagement Index Brands, 2018

Category	Brand
Airlines	Delta
Athletic footwear	Reebok
Coffee (out-of-home)	Dunkin' Donuts and Starbucks (tie)
Energy drinks	Red Bull
Laptop computers	ASUS
Major league sports	MLB
Online retailer	Amazon
Online video streaming	Netflix
Quick-serve restaurants	Chick-fil-A
Search engine	Google
Social networking sites	Facebook and Instagram (tie)
Tablets	Apple
Toothpaste	Colgate
Toys	Lego
Yogurt	Chobani

in table 3.2. You can see the full list at http://brandkeys.com/wp-content/uploads/2018/01/2018-Category-Winners-tableFINAL.pdf.

If any of those loved brands are ones you've used (and chances are, several of them are exactly that), think about how you feel about that brand. Do you love it? If you do, what is it that you love about it? What's your relationship with that brand? And particularly important from a planning perspective, what things has the brand said or done that have helped define your relationship with it?

AAKER'S GUIDELINES FOR STRONG BRANDS

We'll finish this discussion of brands with a list of 10 guidelines for strong brands developed by Dr. David A. Aaker, one of the undisputed branding experts. Aaker has written extensively on brands, including his 1996 classic *Building Strong Brands*. As a planner, you'll be tasked with keeping your brand strong, or helping to make it stronger. So, consider Aaker's 10 guidelines as your to-do list (Aaker, 1996, pp. 356–357):

1. Have a strong brand identity, an image people will remember and respond to.
2. Think carefully about the brand's value proposition, the basic promise it is making to consumers.
3. Develop a clear, easy-to-communicate brand position.

4. Pay attention to how the brand communicates with and to its audience.
5. Keep the brand as consistent as possible over time.
6. Have a coherent brand system, where the different brands in the firm's portfolio make sense relative to one another.
7. Use the brand's identity with care in partnerships, sponsorships, and the like to leverage it in ways that will enhance, not detract from, the brand.
8. Develop and track communications objectives related to the brand to track the brand's equity over time.
9. Assign responsibility for the brand to a specific person who will have the brand as his or her primary focus.
10. Take a long-term view, and continue to invest in the brand even if it may not be meeting all the goals set for it.

The list, particularly the first five elements, could be a job description for a planner. In upcoming chapters, we'll look at some of the other aspects of a planner's job and explore how to go about developing strong brands. But before we move forward, let's hear from another planner. The following comments are from Chelsea St. Clair, cultural strategist, sparks & honey, Los Angeles (https://web.sparksandhoney.com).

What made you want to become a planner/strategist?

I interned at Ogilvy & Mather in 2015, after my junior year. I thought I really wanted to be an account manager but soon after started realizing that wasn't my calling. However, I really enjoyed the environment of an advertising agency and knew that I wanted to be surrounded in this fast-paced world of really smart thinkers. So, I looked around at other disciplines within Ogilvy and shadowed producers, project managers, art buyers, and strategists. I fell in love with the constant learning, the reframing of thinking, and the amazing ideas that are generated and turned into culture-influencing executions. My priority going into strategy was to help change culture through brands, because they have the power and money to effect change.

What do you like most about planning/strategy development?

Pulling insights out of data is surprisingly really fun. I love diving into a set of responses or data sets to pull interesting insights out and weave it into a narrative. I get to spend my days learning, using my critical-thinking skills to help drive the clients and businesses I work with.

What are the characteristics of a great strategist?

Creativity. Intuition. Quick thinker. Self-starter. And when all else fails, a thesaurus.

Perhaps some thoughts about insights from focus groups or in-depth interviews with consumers?

Focus groups, in my opinion, tend to really skew results. In some groups there's common consensus, and instead of gathering really great insights or knowledge you end up getting everyone agreeing. In other groups you have the red herring who really takes away from the relevant conversation and inserts themselves and their opinion on every comment. But IDIs (in-depth interviews) are where it's at. Meet people where they are, make them comfortable, and ask them about the things they love and know well. You'll keep them talking for days and won't have to probe too much because they're so willing to share. Now, of course, getting a client to approve the expense of focus groups or IDIs is a different story.

What's a fun fact or story that you'd like to tell about your experience as a planner?

Not really a fun fact, but being a planner/strategist means that you're always working. When you find something you don't understand, take the time to read, learn, and grasp the concept. When you see your client/product out in the wild, see how people (whether customers or not) interact with it. You're always on the clock because all the things you experience outside of the walls of your office can help influence your insights and thinking for a project you're currently working [on] or that could come up in the future. You're a strategist 24/7 and never forget it.

REFERENCES

Aaker, D. A. (1996). *Building strong brands.* New York, NY: Free Press.

Batra, R., Ahuvia, A., Bagozzi, R. P. (2012, March). Brand love. *Journal of Marketing, 76,* 1–16.

BAV Group. (n.d.). About BAV. Retrieved from https://www.bavgroup.com/about -bav

Bond Brand Loyalty. (2017). The battle for love and loyalty: The loyalty report 2017. Retrieved from http://info.bondbrandloyalty.com/2017-loyalty-report

Brandchannel. (n.d.). Brand glossary: Brand. Retrieved from https://www.brand channel.com/brand-glossary/brand

Brand Keys. (n.d.). Customer loyalty engagement index. Retrieved from http://brandkeys.com/portfolio/customer-loyalty-engagement-index

Edelman. (2017, June). 2017 Edelman Earned Brand study: Beyond no brand's land. Retrieved from https://www.edelman.com/research/earned-brand-2017

Interbrand. (2017). Global Best Brands. Retrieved from https://www.interbrand.com/best-brands/best-global-brands/2017

Interbrand. (n.d.). Methodology. Retrieved from https://www.interbrand.com/best-brands/best-global-brands/methodology

Keller, K. L. (1993). Conceptualizing, measuring, and managing customer-based brand equity. *Journal of Marketing, 57*(1), 1–22.

Lokono. (n.d.). Our story. Retrieved from https://golokono.com/pages/about-us

Lovemarks. (n.d.). About Lovemarks. Retrieved from http://www.lovemarks.com/learn/about

Saatchi & Saatchi Global. (n.d.a). About our network. Retrieved from http://saatchi.com/en-us/network/about

Saatchi & Saatchi Global. (n.d.b). Our clients. Retrieved from http://saatchi.com/en-us/network/clients

Saatchi & Saatchi New York. (n.d.). Our clients. Retrieved from http://saatchiny.com/ny-us/network/clients

Taylor, D. (2017, February 3). A rare trip inside Disney's secret animation vault. *Vulture*. Retrieved from http://www.vulture.com/2017/02/the-disney-vault-is-real-heres-what-its-like-inside.html

TOMS. (n.d.). Improving lives. Retrieved from https://www.toms.com/improving-lives

CHAPTER 4

Marketing Basics Account Planners Need to Know

While advertising is taught in communications or journalism programs in most U.S. universities, it's closely tied to the marketing aspect of business. So, it's important for advertising students to have a sense of how businesses are structured and where marketing fits in to the overall picture as well as knowing the basics of marketing itself. That's what this chapter is about.

BUSINESS STRUCTURE

To look at how businesses are generally set up, consider a major U.S.-based firm, General Mills, as an example. If you're not already familiar with General Mills, they're based out of Minneapolis and own many brands you've probably heard of and used, including Progresso Soup, Cheerios, Yoplait yogurt, and a range of others. They offer products in various product categories (snacks, cereal, convenient meals, yogurt, ice cream, dough, baking mixes, vegetables, and a smattering of others) and have multiple brands in some of those categories (General Mills, 2017).

The company employs people in a number of areas. Those in the corporate area out of Minneapolis are involved in overseeing the range of the business (General Mills sells products in more than 100 countries and has offices in over 30 of them). The engineering area develops processes for manufacturing. Finance handles the monetary side of the business. Human resources provides support for General Mills' 38,000-plus employees. The information technology team works on technology solutions for brands. People in manufacturing produce the products General Mills sells, assisted and overseen by the quality and regulatory operations staff. Those in research and development work on new products and product improvements. The sales team works to get General Mills' brands more exposure.

Supply chain logistics and sourcing people get the raw materials to the production facilities and the finished products out to stores. And the marketing staff oversees everything to do with the brands (General Mills, n.d.b).

The main career area for brand planners has tended to be on the agency side, working in a specialist communication firm. But the brands themselves are generally housed in places like General Mills (i.e., the clients of agencies). It isn't that the people working on the brand from the client side aren't developing strategy. That's a big part of their jobs. However, in most cases, their strategic focus is much broader than that of the agency-based planner. That's because, although advertising and other types of strategic communication are a part of marketing (and often a very expensive part), there's a lot more to marketing than advertising.

MARKETING BASICS

If you've already taken a principles of marketing course, you should know most of the basics. That said, a refresher never hurts. And if you haven't taken such a course or if it's been a while since you were immersed in marketing, what follows are essential points you need to know to provide appropriate support for a brand. It will also help you communicate effectively with your client counterparts.

First, here is the American Marketing Association's definition of marketing: "Marketing is the activity, set of institutions, and processes for creating, communicating, delivering, and exchanging offerings that have value for customers, clients, partners, and society at large" (American Marketing Association, n.d.). *Creating, communicating, delivering,* and *exchanging* are the important words here. You may know those terms better as *product, promotion, place,* and *price,* the four Ps of marketing.

> *Creating* has to do with decisions about the product or service itself: What is it? What's it made of? How is it made? What needs does it meet? How can it be improved? What opportunities are there for new products?
> *Communicating* is the focus of those who work in advertising. What do we need to tell people about the product? How should we tell them? Where should we put those messages?
> *Delivering* is about distribution. How does the brand get to consumers? Where can they find it? From whom do they buy it?
> *Exchanging* is about price, either in dollars and cents or in time. What does the consumer need to give the company in order to get the product or service? Does everyone pay the same price, or does it vary? If it varies, how and why?

That may sound like a fairly simple list, but the issues associated with each of the four areas are complex. As an account planner in an advertising agency, you're focused primarily on the communicating part, but decisions made in the other three areas affect what you do. Also, you need to know at least a little about those other areas in order to understand what goes on with your client. Let's look at each area in more detail.

Product Decisions

One way to think about product decisions is in terms of levels of the product. A commonly used typology looks at the core product, tangible product, and augmented product. The core product is the basic benefit the product provides—that is, its reason for being. Without a good core product, there's no reason to be on the market. And "good" means from the consumer's point of view, so thinking about the core product also means having a good idea of who the competitors are and what each of them is offering in terms of their core product.

When thinking about competitors, it's important to consider both direct competitors (those offering the same type of product) and indirect competitors (those offering a different type of product but one that meets the same basic need). For example, if your client is an automobile manufacturer, other makes and models of cars in a similar price range are your direct competitors, but other transportation options (e.g., public transit, Uber/ Lyft, and even bicycling) are all forms of indirect competition.

The tangible product is the physical product. Questions you ask might be, What does it look like? What is it made of? What colors/flavors/varieties does it come in? Is it environmentally friendly? Does it have unique elements? What's the physical thing customers get when they buy this product or use this service?

The augmented product is any extras that come along with the product. These might include warranties, guarantees, ongoing customer service, upgrade options, or anything additional that is being offered with the product as part of the overall package.

As we saw in the chapter on branding, differentiation is key to building a strong brand. Ideally, that differentiation lies in the core product itself. But when that's not the case, both the tangible product and the augmented product offer other means for setting the brand apart.

Promotion Decisions

This is where advertising comes in to help create and build awareness. Even though a specialist agency (or several) might be involved in crafting the communications, the ultimate responsibility lies with the company behind the brand.

What will the budget for communications be? How will that be allocated across the range of communication techniques being used by the brand, and what will those techniques be? While advertising is critical to the success of most brands, it's generally not the only kind of communication being used. Public relations, sales promotions, direct response, social media, and a range of other techniques might also be part of the mix. As you learned in chapter 2, the POEM model takes into account all these forms of communications as part of the holistic advertising approach. But it's also important to realize that others are also using communications techniques such as the ones mentioned above without considering the advertising strategies being developed at the advertising agency. This is just one more reason that understanding your brand within the entire company is critical.

Another promotion-related decision is whether the focus will be on a push strategy, a pull strategy, or a combination of the two. A push strategy focuses on the distribution channel, so concentrating mainly on wholesalers and retailers to convince them to promote the product to their own customers. In a pull strategy, the majority of the communications attention is on the end user, the consumer. The idea is to convince consumers to buy, so they'll then go in search of the product. Speaking generally, many business-to-business products will tend to use a push strategy, while consumer products are generally focused on pull strategies. Obviously, the type of strategy being used will determine the mix of communications techniques and the specifics of how each technique is applied.

Place Decisions

While distribution decisions have become increasingly complicated due to the rapid increase in direct selling via the Internet, there are three basic distribution strategies: intensive distribution, selective distribution, and exclusive distribution.

In *intensive distribution*, the goal is to have the brand available in all possible outlets where a consumer might look for it—online and in a range of stores (Amazon kiosks in Kohl's, for example). While this is the most expensive distribution strategy, it maximizes the chances of consumers finding the brand rather than being frustrated when it isn't available where they expect it.

Under a *selective distribution* strategy, the brand will be available in multiple places, but there is some picking and choosing involved. For example, a brand like Lululemon operates its own shops in certain markets but also sells through yoga studios as well as working with athletic teams.

An *exclusive distribution* strategy is the most restricted and is usually used to add to the brand's aura of specialness and prestige. For example, there are a number of items in the Martha Stewart Home collection that can only be bought at Macy's department stores.

The brand's chosen distribution strategy affects its advertising, in terms of both media selection and message content. If the brand is being sold through either selective or exclusive distribution, it will be important to include information on where the brand can be found in the advertising. For brands using intensive distribution, it will be important to get the word out about the brand as broadly as possible to maximize sales in support of that intensive distribution. Clearly, it's important that the planner understand which distribution strategy is being used.

Pricing Decisions

As with the other basic elements, there are some accepted strategies used in pricing. Common pricing strategies include market skimming, penetration pricing, economy pricing, and premium pricing. The difference between each of these has to do with the quality of the product as well as the price. In a *market skimming* strategy, the company is trying to sell the product at the highest price the market will accept. In skimming, the quality of the product is often a bit lower than that of other competitors, but the company is counting on consumer interest to generate sales. Skimming strategies are most often used by new products as a way to get initial sales to generate money to support product improvements later.

Penetration pricing is also used by new products. Here, the price of the product is low relative to its quality. A penetration strategy is often tied to an aggressive market share goal. The low price is itself an incentive for consumers to try the product with the hope that a lot of consumers will do just that. If the product is found to be of good quality, consumers might still buy it again at a higher price.

Economy pricing is charging a low price for a product that is also of lower quality than competing products. These are the low-end brands that just about every product category has. For example, Scott Brand paper products tend to be priced lower than many competitive brands in toilet paper and paper towels.

Finally, a *premium* pricing strategy is where a high price is charged for a high-quality product. The price itself is an element of the brand's prestige. Particularly in situations where consumers aren't familiar with a category or don't buy in it often, high price can be taken as an indicator of high quality.

MARKETING JOBS

With that review of marketing basics, let's look more closely at what marketing people do. Let's start by looking at a list of job responsibilities for a position as an associate marketing manager with General Mills. The primary job areas will sound familiar given the discussion above about the components of marketing.

Associate marketing managers help figure out how to achieve the company's business objectives (more on those later in this chapter). They play a role in developing strategies to reach the objectives and are accountable for results; take the lead on pricing decisions and ideas to improve productivity; and lead decisions on packaging, bringing new products to market, and promoting existing product ranges as efficiently as possible. They're expected to constantly track the product's performance and forecast expected future growth while working with people in other parts of the company, including sales, on those projections. They work with outside agencies to execute marketing plans, including advertising and sales promotion programs. And perhaps most important for the planners working with them, they're expected to fully understand the consumer and look for insights that drive purchasing (General Mills, n.d.a).

General Mills also has other types of marketing-related jobs, including positions in marketing communications (generally working with the major retailers the company sells its brands through), creative production management, and marketing capabilities (documenting how the company's successful brands are promoted and sold), as well as other areas.

While General Mills' structure for marketing is fairly standard, it's not the only approach businesses use. Let's look at one more possible organization, from one of the biggest product manufacturers operating in the United States and globally.

Procter & Gamble is a leader in business operations, so they're a good model for a possible structure. P&G groups its brands into 10 Global Business Units: baby care, fabric care, family care, feminine care, grooming, hair care, home care, oral care, personal health care, and skin and personal care (P&G, n.d.b). A separate Selling and Market Operation is organized geographically (Asia Pacific, Europe, Greater China, Latin America, North America and India, the Middle East, and Africa).

There are four brand-focused career areas within the Global Business Unit structure. Those are Brand: Communication, Brand: Consumer & Market Knowledge, Brand: Design, and Brand Marketing/Brand Management (P&G, n.d.a). *Brand: Communication* people focus on the kind of work usually associated with public relations. They're talking about P&G's brands with a range of stakeholders to get more support for the brands and get the brand's messages in front of more people. *Brand: Consumer & Market Knowledge* people identify and analyze trends and try to figure out how to grow P&G's brands by taking a strong consumer perspective. *Brand: Design* people work to come up with ideas for improvements to P&G's brands. And *Brand: Marketing/Brand Management* people are the ones who take the lead on planning how best to further grow P&G's brands by looking at the overall brand picture. Essentially, they're the drivers behind the brand, and they work with people in the other three areas as well as people in outside agencies to make the brand as successful as possible.

In a business with P&G's structure, it's people within the brand management area who have the most to do with strategy, so an agency-based account planner would deal with them most often. The leaders at P&G tend to come out of the brand management side of the business. They have a big-picture view of the brand, dealing with all facets of marketing.

BRAND ARCHITECTURE

Now that you have an understanding of marketing basics and marketing jobs, let's look a bit more closely at how brands work within companies. Many companies have multiple products or services they sell under multiple brands. How those brands are structured within the larger company is known as the *brand architecture*. The best brand architecture systems make it easy for consumers to understand the relationships between the company's different brands, and for the company to introduce new brands that can benefit from the established positive images of its existing brands.

As mentioned earlier, General Mills has more than 100 brands, including multiple brands within the same category. Cereal is one of General Mills' big brand categories. There are 11 brands of General Mills cereal (many with multiple varieties), including Cascadian Farm, Cheerios, Chex, Cinnamon Toast Crunch, Fiber One, Kix, Lucky Charms, Monsters, Total, Trix, and Wheaties. Through that range of brands, General Mills is able to appeal to a number of different consumer segments. For example, Cinnamon Toast Crunch, Kix, Lucky Charms, Monsters (which includes Count Chocula, Franken Berry, and Boo Berry), and Trix primarily appeal to children. Cascadian Farm, Chex, Fiber One, and Total are geared more to adult consumers. Wheaties cuts across both adults and children, through its ties to sports and athletic performance. Cheerios also appeals across age ranges and has a number of line extensions including Honey Nut Cheerios, Multi Grain Cheerios, and Apple Cinnamon Cheerios, among many others.

How do all these cereal brands relate to one another? Most have the General Mills Big G logo prominently displayed on their packaging, so that's one signal to consumers that they're all related. While the look of each brand varies (e.g., logo font and box colors), the look is consistent within each brand's line extensions.

Cascadian Farm is an exception. The General Mills branding isn't prominent with this line of products. Cascadian Farm is an organic company with 75 products branded under its own name. Its ties to General Mills aren't obvious on its website or packaging.

The main range of General Mills' cereals is evidence of a differentiation strategy, where the company offers different products to appeal to multiple consumer segments in order to maximize sales opportunities. The products under the Cascadian Farm name are examples of a focus strategy, narrowing in on the group of consumers who value organic products—and are often willing to pay more for them. General Mills has other organic and natural brands as well, but like Cascadian Farm, those brands are promoted under their own names, with little obvious reference to General Mills.

There are three major types of brand architecture. In a branded house approach, all the company's brands are under the same name. Chevrolet, the auto manufacturer, emphasizes the Chevrolet name and logo on all its makes of cars and trucks. A house of brands approach is where each brand has its own identity and can compete with other brands within the same company. A hybrid or endorsing brand approach is where some brands connect back to the company brand (or master brand), but others don't (Gilman, 2017). That's what General Mills is doing with its cereal brands, connecting the more mainstream brands back to the General Mills name but allowing the organic brands to stand on their own.

OBJECTIVES: FROM BUSINESS TO MARKETING TO ADVERTISING

A lot of what drives the account planner is the objectives set for the brand. What are we trying to accomplish? What are our goals? Objectives get set at many levels, with each higher level affecting the objectives set for the levels below it. The process starts at the very top of the organization, and decisions made early on will affect what the planner needs to accomplish.

All objectives, whatever the level, need to be SMART. The *S* stands for *specific*—objectives should clearly state what you're trying to accomplish. *M* is for *measurable*—good objectives include a numerical goal so that you'll be able to determine if the objective has been accomplished. *A* is for *achievable*—the objectives you set need to be things that can reasonably be accomplished given the resources available. *R* is for *relevant*—the objective needs to make sense in terms of the bigger picture of the business's or brand's success. And *T* is for *time bound*—objectives need to have a specified time frame in which the goal will be achieved.

The three levels of objectives most relevant to our discussion of marketing basics and planning are business objectives, marketing objectives, and advertising objectives.

Business Objectives

Business objectives are the overall goals of the company. Common business objectives focus on areas such as long-term sustainability of the company, revenue generation, cost containment, improved efficiency, and streamlined production. Business objectives usually take a broad view of the entire organization and what it's trying to achieve. Performance against business objectives is the primary focus of top management, boards of directors, and the financial community. Everything that happens within the company is evaluated in terms of how it will help in achieving the business objectives.

For example, General Mills set goals for the 2018 fiscal year in its 2017 annual report involving growth in its cereal and yogurt categories, investing more in its top brands, doing more with natural and organic products, managing its basic brands appropriately, and continuing a restructuring to become a more responsive organization (General Mills, 2017, pp. 5–7). Those business goals would obviously affect the plans for individual brands within the General Mills portfolio. A SMART business objective for General Mills could be, "In the next 12 months, invest in the promotion of our brands to attain the No. 1 market share position in each of the categories in which we compete."

Marketing Objectives

Marketing objectives are usually focused on the specific brand. Common marketing objectives include goals related to sales (either dollar sales or number of units to be sold), market share (performance against competition), return on investment (what the brand makes compared to how much is being spent to produce and sell the brand), distribution (where the brand will be available), and profitability (how much the brand will contribute to the company). Brand and marketing managers on the client side are usually evaluated based on their success at meeting marketing objectives, so those objectives are what they tend to focus on. A SMART marketing objective, then, could be, "In the next 12 months, attain distribution in grocery stores representing 80% of all U.S. grocery sales."

Advertising Objectives

While there are a lot of factors that contribute to a brand's success, as we've seen, advertising is certainly a key player. Advertising objectives are set to map out advertising's role in helping the brand achieve its marketing objectives. Common advertising objectives fall into one of three categories: *cognitive* objectives, *affective* objectives, and *conative* objectives. Cognitive objectives include awareness (how many or what percentage of people in the target audience have heard of the brand) and knowledge (understanding what the brand's about). Affective objectives get into the emotional side of things, such as having a positive attitude toward the brand and preferring the brand to others in the category. Conative objectives are about behavior, encouraging the consumer to want to buy the brand and then actually making a purchase. A SMART advertising objective might be, "In the next six months, educate 65% of our target audience as to the key attributes of our brand." In all cases, objectives should be measurable.

If it all works the way it should, the conative advertising objectives produce the necessary level of sales to meet the marketing objectives. A planner will often be involved in helping set the advertising objectives but also needs to understand that those advertising objectives are driven by the brand's marketing objectives and the overall business objectives. It all ties together.

BRAND MANAGEMENT MATH

If you're like many other advertising students, one reason you're studying advertising instead of being in business school is that you don't consider yourself a numbers person. In this final section of this chapter, however, we need to look at some formulas and numerical concepts you should know and understand to be an effective account planner.

Contribution Margin

We begin with this concept because it is absolutely essential for advertising people. Basically, contribution margin is where the money available to spend on that amazing ad campaign you've developed comes from. Contribution margin is the difference between what it costs to make and distribute the brand and the amount that the company charges for the brand. Once all the costs have been covered, how much money is left over? What makes contribution margin so important is that it's the source of the budget not only for advertising and other types of communication but also for profit. This means that any time you as the advertising person try to convince a brand manager that he or she needs to increase the advertising budget, you had better also have an argument about how that increased budget will lead to increased sales. If you don't, you're essentially saying that the brand's profits will take a hit. (If more is spent on advertising, but only the same amount of product is sold, profits will necessarily go down.) Contribution margin is an easy calculation. What are the cost elements associated with the brand? And what price is charged for the brand? Subtract the former from the latter, and there you are. By the way, you must look at the price the company gets for the product, not what consumers pay in the end. The only time those two prices are the same is when the company sells directly to consumers and doesn't go through any intermediary distribution channels.

Margin

That last sentence above leads to this concept. Margin, or markup, is another way of talking about profit. Many consumer products go from the manufacturer to a wholesaler to a retailer to the consumer. Each of the three entities is involved in getting the product to the consumer. The manufacturer, wholesaler, and retailer each has its own costs and its own business to run. So, each needs to make some money off the deal, or why participate? The amount that gets added at each level is the markup or margin. Obviously, each level wants to maximize its profit, but that's counterbalanced by what competitors are charging and what each level thinks its own customers will be willing to pay. Clearly, it's a trade-off situation. The manufacturer starts the process. Their price will factor in the cost of making and distributing the product as well as profitability goals and the overall pricing strategy, and then there's a ripple effect all the way to the consumer. One important aspect to note here: under U.S. pricing laws, manufacturers don't determine the final price of the product to the consumer except when the manufacturer is selling direct. It's the retailer who sets the price. Manufacturers hope what retailers charge for the product will be in line with the manufacturer's pricing strategy, but retailers will sometimes take a loss on a product to draw more traffic into their stores (called using a loss leader). When eggs sell for 69 cents at your local grocery store, you can be sure you're experiencing a loss leader.

Percentage

Margin is often expressed in terms of a percentage of a markup. To figure the markup, take the price the retailer is charging for the product, subtract the price the retailer paid for the product, and then divide the difference into the price the retailer paid. That's the markup. So, as a hypothetical example, if Publix is charging $1.99 for a can of cat food, and they bought that can from the manufacturer for $1.50, the retailer's markup is about 33%.

Breakeven Analysis and Payout Planning

Breakeven is most often associated with new products, but it can be used anytime a major investment is being made in the brand. In that situation, or with a new product, the company might need to spend more on the brand than it's generating in profits, at least for a period of time. Breakeven analysis looks at those investment costs and determines the point at which the brand's sales will reach a level to repay all the investment and begin to generate a profit. How long a company will be willing to wait for a brand to break even depends on the resources available to support the brand in the meantime. Generally, companies with many already successful brands can afford to be more patient than those with fewer resources.

Return on Investment (ROI)

This is another basic, widely used calculation in marketing. ROI looks at how much the brand is generating compared to how much is being spent on it. To figure this out, you take the brand's sales (in dollars), subtract the cost to make, distribute, and promote the brand, and then divide that result by the total of the combined costs. If we sell $100 worth of product, and it cost us $78 to produce and market that brand, then the return on investment is 28% ($100 – $78 = $22; $22 / $78 = 28%).

Marketing Expense to Revenue

This is another comparison similar to ROI, but this looks specifically at how much is being spent on marketing, primarily on marketing communications, including advertising, and the result from that spending. To calculate this, take the total amount spent on marketing and divide that by the sales revenue. In our previous example, let's say $45 of the $78 in costs was marketing specific. The marketing expense to revenue is then $45 / $100, or 45%.

Customer Acquisition Cost

This calculation looks at the cost to bring a new customer to the brand. If by spending that $45 on marketing the company is able to get 50 new customers, then the customer acquisition cost is 90 cents ($45 / 50).

Lifetime Value

This looks at how much customers might contribute to the brand over the course of the time they use the brand. The higher the lifetime value, the more you might be willing to spend on acquisition cost. For a car manufacturer, you could estimate the number of new cars people might buy during their driving life and multiply that times the average cost of a new car from your line. That's the estimated lifetime value.

As you can see, basic marketing math is just addition, subtraction, multiplication, and division—basic. Spend some time getting to understand the reasoning behind the numbers as well as how to figure them out, and you'll find yourself able to speak with your marketing counterparts with much greater confidence.

With that review of marketing basics, it's now time to turn to a topic at the core of the account planner's job—understanding the consumer.

SUGGESTED ACTIVITIES
TO HELP YOU THINK ABOUT THIS CHAPTER

Activity 1: Think about a place where you have either worked or interned. Try to figure out the business structure of that company. Describe as many different positions at that company that you can remember. How did these positions interact with each other?

Activity 2: Who was the competition—both direct and indirect—for the company you described in activity 1? How does that competition affect your company?

Activity 3: What do the marketing people do at this company? Do they work with an advertising agency? If so, how do they interact? If they don't work in an advertising agency, do they have an in-house agency? If so, how is it set up compared to a traditional advertising agency?

REFERENCES

American Marketing Association. (n.d.). Definition of Marketing. Retrieved from https://www.ama.org/the-definition-of-marketing

General Mills. (2017). 2017 annual report. Retrieved from https://s22.q4cdn .com/584207745/files/doc_financials/2017/annual/General-Mills-2017-Annual -Report.pdf

General Mills. (n.d.a). Careers: Associate marketing manager. Retrieved from https://careers.generalmills.com

General Mills. (n.d.b). Talent areas. Retrieved from https://careers.generalmills.com /talent-areas

Gilman, S. (2017, March 31). What is brand architecture? Gravity Group. Retrieved from https://www.gravitygroup.com/blog/what-is-brand-architecture

P&G. (n.d.a). Career areas. Retrieved from https://www.pgcareers.com/career-areas

P&G. (n.d.b). Structure and governance. Retrieved from https://us.pg.com/who-we -are/structure-governance/corporate-structure

CHAPTER 5

Who Is Your Target Audience?

As you'll remember from chapter 1, one of the key responsibilities of the account planner is understanding the audience and what motivates them so that you, the planner, can be the voice of the consumer within the agency. That requires a depth of understanding of the people you're trying to persuade through the advertising campaign, and much of this book explores ways of developing that understanding. But before we get to the *how*, we need to focus on the *who*.

TARGET MARKET VERSUS TARGET AUDIENCE

Think back to our discussion of the various levels of objectives in the previous chapter. You can't set advertising objectives without thinking about the person you're trying to communicate with. Sometimes, target market and target audience are used interchangeably, but they are really two distinct concepts. Target market is the broader of the two, while target audience is an important subset. The account planner is keenly focused on the target audience.

Target Market

The target market is the segment of people that the company intends to focus on to sell its product or service. Target market segments are usually described in terms of a combination of factors including demographics, geographics, psychographics, and usage. Common demographic considerations include gender, age, income, occupation, education, race, and family size. Geographics include region of the country and type of locality (e.g., center cities, suburbs, small towns, and rural areas). Client firms and agencies use large annual national surveys like those conducted by GfK

MRI (mri.gfk.com) and Simmons Research (https://www.simmonsresearch
.com) to identify the demographic and geographic characteristics of current
users of various brands.

Psychographics have to do with people's lifestyles—their hobbies, leisure
pursuits, attitudes, and opinions. GfK MRI and Experian Simmons also include information on media use (this is a main way those surveys are used,
to choose media to reach specific target audiences), and that can be used
to make inferences about psychographics. For example, people who read
several travel magazines most likely enjoy traveling, while people reading
magazines about hunting, fishing, and hiking typically spend much of their
free time outdoors.

Another tool for getting at psychographics is VALS, a framework developed by Strategic Business Insights (SBI; http://www.strategicbusinessin-
sights.com/vals). VALS stands for *values, attitudes,* and *lifestyles.* The VALS
typology classifies people into one of eight segments based on mind-set.
There are two main components to VALS: the person's level of resources (including relative wealth, age, and education) and health status, energy level,
and leadership qualities (classified as either high or low). VALS also looks at
a person's primary motivation. There are three primary motivations: ideals,
achievement, and self-expression. People motivated by ideals are driven
by their principles and operate based on knowledge. People motivated by
achievement are concerned about how they are viewed by other people.
People motivated by self-expression are looking for variety, might be more
willing to take risks, and are focused on activity. You can read about each of
the eight VALS types and take a quiz to see the type (or types) you fall into
on the SBI website noted above.

Some target market descriptions include geo demographics, a combination of geographic and demographic information. One example of this is
Claritas PRIZM. PRIZM puts households in the United States into 1 of 66
different segments based on socioeconomic, life stage, and social factors.
On the PRIZM website (segmentationsolutions.nielsen.com), you can put
in your zip code and see which PRIZM segments you and your neighbors
fall into. For example, five PRIZM segments are represented within the
40515 zip code in Lexington, Kentucky:

- 03 Movers and Shakers (wealthy, older, mostly without kids)
- 06 Winner's Circle (wealthy, middle age, mostly with kids)
- 14 Kids and Cul-de-Sacs (upscale, younger, family mix)
- 22 Middleburg Manager (upscale, middle age, family mix)
- 48 Generation Web (low income, middle age, family mix)

Usage considerations include amount of brand use within a specified
period of time such as the last six months or the past week and whether

a group is brand loyal or not (defined based on how often people in the group choose the specific brand versus competitors). These and other factors are used to define a target market.

So, the target market for General Mills' Honey Nut Cheerios, based on current users, might be defined as women between the ages of 35 and 44 who attended college and have a household income of between $60,000 and $74,999, have kids ages 13 to 16 living at home and living in the northeastern United States, and are concerned about healthy yet delicious eating. That certainly helps us start to focus on who we need to talk to in our advertising, but there's still a great deal of variability in that group, and not all women in that target market are likely to really pay attention to our ads for Honey Nut Cheerios, no matter how good we think they are. (By the way, if you're wondering why the target market isn't kids, it's not the kids who buy the cereal. It's their moms.)

Target Audience

That brings us to the target audience, a subgroup within the larger target market. The target audience is made up of the people within the target market who are most likely to respond to our advertising. The target audience description takes the characteristics used to identify the target market and adds a deeper consumer understanding into the mix. Getting to the deeper understanding is a crucial job for the account planner. We'll be looking at some of the research tools and techniques that can be used to help uncover that deeper understanding in the next few chapters. For now, let's look further at defining the target audience.

What we're really trying to do is get as close as possible to being able to picture a specific person (or a couple, or group, depending on the brand) who is most likely to be receptive to the advertising we'll create for the brand. For Honey Nut Cheerios, that specific target audience might well be a mom and her kids. We want to think about who they are on a day-by-day basis. What's breakfast time like in their home? Is everyone sitting down together around the table, or is it a grab your bowl, eat, and go kind of breakfast? Is mom getting ready to head to work while the kids head to school? How and where does Honey Nut Cheerios fit in to all this? So as you can see, while the target market might be women ages 35–44 living in the Northeast with kids aged 13–16 at home, the target audience might be women 35–44 and their kids aged 13–16 living in the Northeast who need a good, enjoyable, quick, and easy-to-prep breakfast to get the day started right.

PERSONAS

An important tool planners use to think about the target audience is personas. Think of the persona as a representative of the target audience. In developing the persona, the planner zooms in on that mom and kids introduced above. Who are they, really? That description will include demographic and geographic information, but it will also go deeper.

As you may have already guessed, psychographics are one of the most important elements in moving from a broad target market to a much more specific target audience. Really getting a sense of people's lifestyles can unlock a far deeper understanding of who they really are and what motivates them. Tools like VALS and other psychographic segmentation models can be very helpful, but always, always remind yourself that you're talking about real people, not groups or numbers. What is this person's life really like? What matters most to this person? That's what you need to get to as you develop the persona.

Thinking about our cereal-eating family, what are their aspirations, their hopes, and their fears? How do they like to spend their free time? What kinds of things do they do together, and when do they like to be on their own, away from the others? What do they care about? The persona will help you, and the creative team, think about this target audience in a rich, personal way, and that will make it much easier to develop advertising ideas that will directly speak to them.

Here's a possible persona description for our Honey Nut Cheerios family. (By the way, the most useful personas often include a lot of visuals, which we've not done here.)

Susan Allison is a 38-year-old woman living in Manchester, New Hampshire. Susan and her husband, Joe, have three daughters, Lynn (age 16), Paige (14), and Grace (13). Susan and Joe both work full time, and Susan's an event planner for a local college. The girls are all involved in sports. Lynn and Grace are soccer players, and Paige plays softball. Lynn's close to getting her driver's license but is not quite there yet. Susan and Joe (Susan especially) are both counting the days until Lynn can start driving and help transport herself and her sisters to all their activities.

Susan spends a lot of time juggling Joe's and the girls' activities as well as her own. (She loves going out with her girlfriends once a week, does scrapbooking, and likes to cook when she has time.) She's not a penny pincher, but she does look for deals, and she's willing to give store brands a try as long as the quality is good. Convenience is really important to her because it helps her with time management.

The easiest thing for all the Allisons would be if they all liked the same foods, but they don't. They agree on some snacks, but Joe and Grace like spicier food than do the others, while Lynn and Paige both like sweets. Susan's not a stickler for things being healthy, but she'd prefer that they all be eating with at least a little bit of an eye on whether things are good for them or not. Susan's mom cooked a lot while she was growing up, and Susan always has a little voice in the back of her head reminding her about how good those home-cooked meals were. So, while she likes convenience and saving money, neither of those are priorities over helping keep the family in decent shape by buying good food.

Lynn has been studying nutrition in school and has started to get on the rest of the family about their healthy eating habits or, more accurately, the lack thereof. Susan's willing to listen to some of Lynn's suggestions on what they should all be eating, but she also has pointed out to Lynn that it doesn't matter if it's good for you if you don't like the taste.

Many personas are much more detailed than this, but you get the idea. You want to have a realistic person in mind so you can better understand what kinds of things might motivate your target audience. It's also important to understand that persona descriptions are based on research you've uncovered. While the description might sound as if it came from someone with a vivid imagination, in reality, the persona was developed from hours of creative research, which you'll learn more about in later chapters.

CUSTOMER JOURNEY MAPPING

Another tool that can help planners get a deeper sense of the target audience is customer journey mapping. This is a concept originally developed by website designers who were mapping out how site users might move through online content. The customer journey map gave them insights into such things as what order content should be in and what should be linked where. It's also a guide to frustrations site users might run into in trying to find the information they're looking for.

The adaptation to other marketing situations starts by looking at the decision-making process the target audience, or more helpfully, a persona, would go through in moving toward purchasing the product. The traditional decision-making process is problem recognition (realizing there's a difference between where you are and where you want to be), information search (looking for possible solutions to the problem), evaluation of alternatives (weighing the different possible solutions against each other), purchase (picking one alternative and buying it), and postpurchase evaluation (looking at how good a choice you made). A customer journey map can use that basic process or adapt it as appropriate.

Next, for each step in the process, you put yourself into the persona's mind-set (so the better the understanding you have of that persona, the easier it will be for you to do this). What's their goal at each step along the way? What questions are they trying to answer?

Given the goals at each step, what are the brand touchpoints that might come into play? In other words, how and where can we place Honey Nut Cheerios into the equation?

Then, it's important to think about what frustrations or challenges the persona might encounter at each stage. What might go wrong?

Finally, given what we've learned, what changes can or should we, the brand, make in what we're doing in order to better meet the needs of the persona?

That may all sound a bit abstract. A basic, very simple customer journey map for our mom, Susan, and the girls when it comes to breakfast choices in general and Honey Nut Cheerios in particular can be found in table 5.1.

POSITIONING

We have one more concept before we wrap up our look at target audiences. A positioning statement is a one-sentence summary of the relationship between the target audience and the brand. While there are some different ways to phrase a positioning statement, we particularly like one developed by Chris Kocek in *The Practical Pocket Guide to Account Planning* (2013, p. 103). His format is, "For [target audience who _____], [your brand] is the only one that delivers [benefit/point of difference] because only [your brand] is [reason to believe]." Here's a possible positioning statement for Honey Nut Cheerios based on our personas and the customer journey map:

> For women aged 35–44 and their teen kids who are concerned about healthy eating, Honey Nut Cheerios is the only one that delivers both good taste and good nutrition because only Honey Nut Cheerios has whole grain oats plus sweet honey.

There are a range of possibilities, or positioning approaches, to draw on for the point of difference. Here are some commonly used positioning approaches, with examples for Honey Nut Cheerios:

- *Positioning based on product attributes.* Honey Nut Cheerios is unique because of the combination of honey, whole grains, and almonds.
- *Positioning based on competitors.* Honey Nut Cheerios is a healthier choice than other sweetened breakfast cereals.
- *Positioning based on use/application.* Honey Nut Cheerios is a sweet, healthy afternoon snack.
- *Positioning based on the price/quality relationship.* Honey Nut Cheerios is good value for the cost.

Table 5.1. Allison Family Customer Journey Map

Decision-making Stage	Problem Recognition	Information Search	Evaluation of Alternatives	Purchase	Postpurchase Evaluation
Audience goal	Need a healthier breakfast (than waffles, cinnamon rolls, etc.) that everyone will like	What options are convenient, good for you, and liked by everyone?	Narrowed down to cold cereal because of convenience factor with everyone's schedules. Which one is best?	Give Honey Nut Cheerios a try—honey and nuts should be tasty, and oats are good for you.	Does everyone like it? And does it really seem healthier?
Touchpoints	Lynn's comments on what's wrong with what they're eating now	Lynn's nutrition teacher's recs. Friends' comments on what they/their kids like. Looking in the breakfast section of the grocery.	TV and print ads for cereals. Cereal boxes in the store. Cereal websites. Google results for "healthy cereal" that sound as if it might taste OK.	In-store experience (package, design, price, shelf position)	Product taste, nutrition information on the box
Challenges	Lynn says what's wrong but doesn't have a lot of ideas on options. Is there something that will work for them all?	Lots of options. It's hard to sort through them all, especially to find something to satisfy both the health aspect and a sweet tooth.	Still a lot to choose from, and what's healthy enough to satisfy Lynn might not taste that good.	Not always easy to find a particular cereal among all the others. Others may be less expensive.	If it tastes good, can it really be healthy? Are there other options that are healthier or less expensive (or both)?
Possible changes	Honey Nut Cheerios isn't on the radar yet. Sponsor kids' teams to increase awareness.	Promote both health benefits and taste.	Make sure website highlights both taste and health. Do sampling in-store and at events to demonstrate taste claims.	Evaluate package graphics to make sure it stands out on the shelf. Use point-of-purchase displays.	Provide incentives for continued purchase, such as coupons in the box. Highlight social media platforms on box to encourage engagement.

- *Positioning based on product user.* Honey Nut Cheerios is a good breakfast choice for moms and kids.
- *Positioning based on product class.* Honey Nut Cheerios is a good-tasting, healthy cereal.

For Susan and her girls, it's the combination of good taste and decent nutrition that's most important, so positioning on product attributes makes the most sense. That positioning also speaks to most of the concerns identified in the customer journey map. But how do you know which positioning approach makes the most sense for your brand?

As with everything else, it starts with that target audience. What's the most important thing to them? Yet it's also very important to think about positioning in regard to your competitors. One of the earliest in-depth looks at positioning was Al Ries and Jack Trout's *Positioning: The Battle for Your Mind*, first published in 1981. They described how consumers perceive competing brands within a product category and how brands can best "position" themselves for success. So, when you're considering the different approaches to positioning a brand you're working on, think about your target audience, but also look closely at what your competitors are saying and doing. You want a position your brand can own, one that will differentiate you from all the other options.

So, how do account planners get the information they need to understand the customer and the brand? They do so through a range of research techniques, which we'll explore in the next four chapters.

SUGGESTED ACTIVITIES
TO HELP YOU THINK ABOUT THIS CHAPTER

Activity 1: Think of a brand your grandparents might use that you don't. Write a target market description for that brand including demographics, geographics, psychographics, and usage characteristics. (If you have access to GfK MRI or Simmons Research, you can pull the information from there, but if not, just do this based on your own knowledge and assumptions.)

Activity 2: A *persona* paints a picture of your target audience with words. Write a persona for the brand you chose that your grandparents might use. Include a photo of a single person who visually represents your target audience.

Activity 3: Finally, keeping the persona you developed in mind, create a customer journey map for the brand you chose, following the example in table 5.1.

REFERENCES

Kocek, C. (2013). *The practical pocket guide to account planning.* Austin, TX: Yellow Bird Press.

Ries, A., & Trout, J. (1981). *Positioning: The battle for your mind.* New York: Mc-Graw-Hill.

CHAPTER 6

Secondary Research

No Matter What, Do This First!

Now that you have a sense of some of the fundamentals of account planning and the account planner's role, as well as the basics of branding and understanding the target audience, it's time to look at some of the tools used by account planners. While many advertising agencies no longer have formal research departments (at least, not large ones), that doesn't mean research is ignored. In fact, it's absolutely essential, particularly for account planners. After all, how can a planner understand the environment the brand is operating in and, most critically, who the brand's consumers are and what motivates them—the all-important insight—without research?

There are two basic types of research: secondary research and primary research. Primary research further subdivides into quantitative and qualitative methods, which we'll look at in the next few chapters. But for now, our focus is on secondary research. While it's called "secondary," as the chapter title says, it's what comes first.

Secondary research draws on information sources that already exist rather than constructing your own research study. There is a wealth of information available for almost any product category, and in our wired world, it's easier than ever to locate and access that information. Secondary research always comes first because it's quick, easy, and much less expensive than primary research. There's no need to reinvent the wheel if someone else has already looked at the question you're trying to answer. Secondary research is the true workhorse in many campaigns, especially when the planner is working on a new business pitch where time and budget are tight.

When you begin to work with a brand, you need to immerse yourself in that brand, learning as much about it as possible. You want to use it yourself (assuming that's an option), but you also want to read, watch, and listen to everything you can find on it. Look at information from the company itself, but also look at what other people have said about that brand. What have journalists said about it? Industry insiders? Competitors? Customers? All of this is secondary research, and all of it can help you develop a deeper understanding of the brand, and then give you some direction on moving from understanding to insight.

ORGANIZING SECONDARY DATA

Once you've gathered your secondary data, what do you do with it to organize it in a way that will truly be helpful? There are some basic, widely used approaches, each of which is briefly discussed below.

SWOT Analysis

We mentioned SWOT briefly in chapter 1. Here's a little more about what it is and how it works. SWOT stands for strengths, weaknesses, opportunities, and threats, and it's a convenient and helpful way to organize a variety of information on a brand or company. The strengths and weaknesses are things internal to the brand. Strengths are what it does particularly well in terms of meeting consumer needs, quality, performance relative to competition, and other such things. Weaknesses are the problem areas, things that need improvement, such as quality consistency and distribution, among others. Opportunities and threats are things outside the brand's direct control that can affect how it operates. They are often characteristics of the overall product category and can also include such things as the regulatory climate and economic environment. Opportunities are the positive trends that might be capitalized on, and threats are the negatives that need to be monitored. A SWOT analysis is often visualized as a two-by-two table with bullet points along with an accompanying narrative that goes into more detail on each point (including the source of each piece of information).

SOAR Analysis

SOAR stands for strengths, opportunities, aspirations, and results. SOAR is a more forward-looking, planning-focused approach than a SWOT analysis. SOAR doesn't look at weaknesses but instead focuses on what the brand or company is doing well (the strengths), things it might capitalize on (opportunities), where it wants to go (aspirations), and what should be looked at to determine success (results). Where a SWOT can be developed by an outsider (such as an account planner or account planner-to-be), a SOAR is usually done internally drawing on multiple voices within the organization.

Situation Analysis

A situation analysis looks at the brand's current situation. It includes discussion of the product or service itself including distribution and pricing, competition (who the competitors are and what they have to offer compared to our brand), legal and political climate affecting the brand, and current advertising and other communication elements. It's not unusual to summarize a situation analysis with a SWOT analysis.

Brand Business Review

This type of analysis is often broader than a situation analysis. It usually has a stronger focus on both the brand and the consumer as well as looking at the elements in a situation analysis.

Brand Audit

This is all about the brand. A brand audit takes a close look at every element of the brand, including not only the physical product or service but also the logo and other imagery pertaining to the brand, all of the brand's communication touchpoints, positioning, and everything that contributes to the brand image. One of the major goals of a brand audit is to assess how well the brand is performing based on its stated objectives. The audit helps identify any areas that need to be improved or modified.

Whichever approach (or approaches) you choose to use, the key is to go through all the information you've gathered looking for common themes. An issue that's mentioned in only one place isn't as important as one you see discussed from multiple sources. You need to be able to sort through all the data and figure out what's most relevant to the problem you're trying to solve. One of the skills that good account planners have is the art of synthesis—that is, being able to pull together information from multiple sources into a cohesive, analytical whole. It's the critical and analytical thinking ability that's mentioned in so many job ads and surveys of what employers are looking for. Training yourself to become a good secondary researcher is one way to further develop your skills in this area.

With that background on the role and use of secondary research, we'll now introduce you to some of the most widely used secondary sources, including major sources that advertising agencies and marketing firms expect their employees to know about. Most often, you'd be doing secondary research on a specific topic (a brand, an industry, or a particular audience segment, for example), but many of the sources we'll cover here are things you should bookmark and look at regularly to keep up to date with what's going on in the overall industry.

WHAT KINDS OF
QUESTIONS CAN SECONDARY RESEARCH ANSWER?

You can use secondary sources to determine a brand's current sales, its market share, how much it's spending on advertising and where that money is going, its current creative campaign, the agency or agencies working with the brand, and answers to many other questions a planner might ask to get a strong sense of the brand.

Let's look first at one of the broadest groups of information, the articles and studies indexed in several widely used search databases. There are many options, but here are four that should be available through most libraries' online resources.

ABI Inform (https://www.proquest.com/products-services/abi_inform_global.html). ABI Inform is a product of ProQuest. This database covers academic journals as well as periodicals in business and economics. ABI Inform includes Experian information on a large number of companies, which is useful when putting together brand and competitor profiles.

Business Source Complete (https://www.ebsco.com/products/research-databases/business-source-complete). Business Source Complete, a product of EBSCO, indexes a wide range of business-focused journals and magazines. It's a comprehensive source for finding articles in the trade press on particular brands, industries, and other business topics. The resource also gives you access to Associated Press video. There's a Company View feature that provides basic information (including financial information) on a large number of both privately held and public companies.

LexisNexis (https://www.lexisnexis.com/en-us/products/nexis.page). LexisNexis originated as a database for legal cases but then branched out into other areas. The Nexis aspect is the one most relevant to our interests. Nexis indexes articles from 40,000+ sources, including articles from many newspapers. Newspaper business sections often include profile articles on local companies. Those can be an excellent source of basic information, including sales and other financial data.

Readers' Guide to Periodical Literature (https://www.ebsco.com/products/research-databases/readers-guide-periodical-literature). This is another EBSCO product. It primarily indexes consumer magazines. While it might not lead you to data on a brand's sales or market share, it might point you to articles that will help you understand how consumers view the brand and how highly regarded it is.

Here are a few tips when using ABI Inform, Business Source Complete, Nexis, or the Readers' Guide. In our field, you have to deal with current information. Consumer interests change, sales are affected by forces within and beyond the company's control, new products come on the market, and old ones are discontinued. Therefore, when you start, use the search tools in each database to limit your search to the past six months. If that time frame doesn't give you the information you're hoping for, extend it to one year, and so on. Just keep in mind that the older the article, the less likely it is to be relevant.

Similarly, keep the geography of your client's brand in mind. If the client wants you to look only at its U.S. business, then you need to be dealing with U.S. sources. All four databases let you choose geography. But if your client sells outside the United States, it wouldn't hurt to get an idea of what's going on with the brand elsewhere in the world. Just keep your primary focus on U.S. sources.

On a related note, keep an eye on what sources you choose to use. If you come across an article from a publication or other source you've not heard of before, check it out. Go to its website (and if it doesn't have one, wonder why that's the case), read about it, and make sure it's legitimate. Confidence in the source of the information is an important aspect of secondary research use. That's why you'll see us providing information on the methodology behind the sources we're recommending in most cases. It matters where information comes from and how it's collected. As an account planner, it's your responsibility to know the quality of the information you're basing your decisions on, so get in the habit of verifying the sources you use.

Statista (statista.com) is another compendium site with lots of useful information on a range of topics. Statista draws on more than 22,000 sources for its information and covers more than 80,000 topics dealing with 170 industries (Statista, n.d.a). In addition to a tremendous amount of basic information, Statista is known for its Digital Market Outlook reports that focus on a range of digital sectors: digital media, e-commerce, FinTech, e-services, digital advertising, smart home, connected car, and e-travel (Statista, n.d.b). If you're working on a brief in any of those areas, Statista is definitely the place to start, but the site can help with most any traditional market as well.

Consumer Research

There are two major, national syndicated research studies conducted annually that look at both people's buying behavior and media usage. The two companies involved in this work are GfK MRI and Simmons Research.

GfK MRI (https://mri.gfk.com) produces the Survey of the American Consumer. This study looks at consumers' self-reported purchasing of thousands of brands across a range of close to 600 product and service categories. Study participants are also asked about their media use for print media (about 225 titles), broadcast and cable TV networks, and radio formats and networks, as well as other media use. All this is tied to demographic data including gender, age, occupation, income, race, family size and age(s) of children, and region. The survey is sold to ad agencies and marketing firms. There's also a version that universities can subscribe to, providing access to year-old data. The survey is administered face-to-face in people's homes, and 25,000 American consumers are interviewed.

Simmons Research (n.d.) produces the Simmons National Consumer Study. This one looks at 500+ product categories, major media use, and more than 1,000 media vehicles, and also asks about consumers' attitudes and opinions on a range of topics. The Simmons study also includes 25,000 U.S. adults, selected using a patented sample design. It also is a subscription service and is used widely in the advertising industry.

Another aspect to consumer research where secondary sources can be helpful is to find out how consumers feel about the brand, what they've been told about it, and how they're talking about it. The Readers' Guide mentioned above can certainly help with that, but so can a much more recently available information source—the range of social listening tools that have been developed to help monitor social media conversations. There are a *lot* of them, some platform specific, others working across social media platforms. Many charge for their services (understandably), but many are either completely free or have a less sophisticated free version. You'll learn about some of the most popular ones in chapter 7.

Media Research

Information on media research sources would fill a book on its own (and there are quite a few books on the topic). But you might want to get an idea of the reach and possible impact of your brand's advertising or that of your competitors. The GfK MRI and Experian Simmons studies mentioned earlier include a lot of media usage information. In addition, each major media type has an advertising-focused organization associated with it (e.g., Outdoor Advertising Association of America, News Media Alliance for newspapers, and Association of Magazine Media). Each of those organization's websites includes a great deal of data on advertising trends as well as research studies on how that type of media can be used most effectively.

If you're curious about television program ratings, check out TV by the Numbers (https://tvbythenumbers.zap2it.com). Its ratings section has daily and weekly ratings information across broadcast, cable, and syndicated TV, as well as DVR information.

The TV by the Numbers data come from the Nielsen company (http://www.nielsen.com/us/en.html). TV ratings are what most Americans know

Nielsen for, but the company also does audience measurement for other types of media, including online. They are also a major market research firm, operating in a variety of industries. The Insights section of their website (http://www.nielsen.com/us/en/insights.html) has a wide range of fascinating reports on audience segments, product categories, buyer behavior, you name it. It's well worth signing up for their electronic newsletter to get updates when new reports are issued.

SOCIAL MEDIA RESEARCH

In addition to the social listening tools discussed later in chapter 7, there are some other sources of information on social media worth knowing about. First, every major social media platform has information geared for businesses and nonprofits to help those kinds of organizations make the best use of the platform. You can easily find these by doing a search engine hunt using "[name of social media platform] for business" (e.g., Instagram for business or Twitter for business). Because those sites are also designed to convince companies to spend money on that particular search engine, they usually have statistics on the platform's users and usage characteristics.

Socialbakers (https://www.socialbakers.com) is a site that monitors a number of social media platforms. The free portion of the Socialbakers site has information on Facebook, Twitter, and YouTube, including up to six months of historical data. Paid Socialbakers subscribers get those three plus LinkedIn, Instagram, Pinterest, and VKontakte, a Russian platform, with up to five years of historical data.

For the three free-access platforms, Socialbakers provides global and country-by-country data on users and most popular pages in the categories of brands, celebrities, communities, entertainment, media, place, society (including politicians), and sport. Socialbakers also publishes monthly social marketing reports with basic information on the major platforms.

Comscore (https://www.comscore.com) is a business providing audience measurement data across a range of platforms. It looks at TV viewing, digital use, and movie viewing around the world. Much of what they do is proprietary, but Comscore does publish frequent reports and insights on a variety of media and advertising topics, including social and mobile media.

The Pew Research Center (http://www.pewresearch.org) conducts wide-ranging research related to many of the topics marketers and advertisers care about. Pew's topic areas include U.S. politics, media and news, social trends, religion, Internet and technology, science, Hispanics, and global. Pew's Internet and technology studies include a number of reports dealing with social media use. The social trends area often has studies that can really help a planner understand different audience segments more deeply. Like many of the other resources we've mentioned, Pew offers the opportunity to sign up for regular email newsletters to keep up to date on its latest research.

IHS Markit (formerly Polk; https://ihsmarkit.com) provides its subscribers with detailed data on a range of industries, including automotive, energy and natural resources, and financial services, among others. They frequently issue news releases highlighting some of their research, and those can include useful information for planners. This is one you'll likely come across if you're working for an agency that has clients in one of IHS Markit's focus fields.

Maritz CX (https://www.maritzcx.com) specializes in customer experience research, looking at how consumers engage and interact with companies. Most of what they offer is restricted to their own customers, but they're another organization that puts out press releases on some of their work. This is another information provider you're likely to encounter in an agency setting.

COMPANY SOURCES

While it's important to get an independent read on how a brand or company is doing from journalists and other industry observers, the company itself can be a useful information source, particularly if it's publicly traded. That's because the U.S. Securities and Exchange Commission (SEC) requires that companies regularly provide their shareholders and the investment community with performance updates.

Quarterly reports, as the name suggests, are filed every three months. These reports go to the SEC but are also shared with investors. Quarterly reports are focused on financial information and include operating expenses, cash flow, gross revenue, and net profit. Basically, they provide a snapshot of the company's financial health.

Annual reports cover the entire year. While they include financial information, they often also review major events of the preceding year and the company's goals, and may highlight particular brands or other key aspects of the company's business. The primary audience for the annual report is the company's shareholders, which is one of the reasons an annual report is usually quite detailed. Most companies will have a section on its website for investors, and that's where both annual and quarterly reports can be found. A helpful note: If it isn't in the top menu bar, check at the bottom of the home page.

Another type of report that may be provided by a company, and one that can yield especially useful information for planners, is a corporate social responsibility report. CSR (or CSI, for corporate social investment or initiatives) is the doing-good side of the company, the causes and programs it supports. This is an increasingly important area for many businesses, at least in part because consumers, and Millennials in particular, are more interested in how firms are giving back. CSR reports generally include examples of where the company is trying to make a difference, and those may reveal useful angles for consumer insights to drive brand consideration and purchasing.

Finally, most companies also maintain a newsroom or pressroom section on their websites. This is where press releases are archived, and in some cases, there are also links to news stories on the company.

When using company sources, just keep in mind that, like advertising, the intent is generally to make the company look good. While it's fine to use information directly from the company, *you want to balance that with information from outside sources.*

ANNUAL STUDIES

This next group of resources is ongoing, yearly studies issued by some of the leading agencies in the advertising, branding, and marketing communications fields. The trends identified in these various studies can be especially helpful in looking for consumer motivations and developing insights. Plus, they just make for interesting reading.

Best Brands (https://www.interbrand.com/best-brands). We introduced this study in chapter 3. The 2017 Global version was based on financial data from Thomson Reuters, consumer data from Canadean (now GlobalData), social media information from Twitter, and social media analysis from Infegy. The report includes a profile of each brand in the top 100, including the historical trend of its brand value and its social impact based on likes and people talking about the brand on Facebook and followers on Twitter. To the extent that your brand or its major competitors are in the top 100, this is a quick source of basic data.

Brand Z (http://www.brandz.com). Brand Z, a division of Kantar Millward Brown research, issues a yearly ranking of the top 100 most valuable global brands. The rankings come from interviews with consumers (more than 3 million consumers for the 2018 ranking) as well as financial analysis based on data from Kantar Worldpanel and Bloomberg.

Customer Loyalty Engagement Index (http://brandkeys.com/portfolio /customer-loyalty-engagement-index). The Brand Keys Customer Loyalty Engagement Index was also mentioned in chapter 3. For the 2018 study, Brand Keys conducted a combination of telephone, online, and face-to-face interviews with more than 50,500 U.S. consumers aged 16–65. The study participants only rated brands that they themselves consume.

Earned Brand (https://www.edelman.com/earned-brand). Earned Brand comes from Edelman. Edelman began its life as a public relations agency, growing to become the largest independent agency in the world. They now classify themselves as a global communications marketing firm and look at a range of areas beyond traditional PR. Earned Brand looks at people's trust in, expectations of, and relationships with brands. The most recent study, conducted in 2017, is based on online interviews with 14,000 respondents in 14 countries as well as an analysis of social media conversations.

Edelman Trust Barometer (https://www.edelman.com/trust-barometer). The Edelman Trust Barometer has been running since 2001. It looks at public trust in four major institutions: nongovernmental organizations, business, government, and the media. For the 2018 study, more than 33,000 consumers over the age of 18 living in more than 25 markets around the world participated in an online survey.

Most Loved Brands (https://morningconsult.com/most-loved-brands). This annual study from Morning Consult Polling is based on interviews with adults in the United States. For the 2018 study, Morning Consult used online surveying to get input on a wide range of brands from more than 250,000 adults. The primary measure is a net favorability score, where the percentage of people who rate the brand unfavorably is subtracted from the percentage who rate it favorably. For example, Google is number 1 on the 2018 list, with a net favorability score of 78.7.

ALL-AROUND PLANNING RESOURCES

Lovemarks Campus (http://www.lovemarkscampus.com). Lovemarks Campus is a website developed to help spread the gospel of Saatchi & Saatchi's Lovemarks concept that we saw in chapter 3. In addition to some Lovemarks-specific information, this website has a Resources section that collects interesting research studies from Saatchi & Saatchi personnel and others. It's another one to bookmark as you build your planning toolbox.

Planners Dilemma (http://plannersdilemma.misentropy.com). This is a one-stop shop for a wide range of articles about planning, examples of multiple creative briefs, and a long list of planning tools with links to each of them. While the nature of the information here may be more helpful when you're developing a primary research study, this site is a valuable resource for current and aspiring planners.

You won't necessarily use all the resources we've described every time you're beginning to work on a brand; what you'll need depends on the particular problem you've been asked to address. But having a repertoire of secondary tools is a very important part of the planner's resource set.

SUGGESTED ACTIVITIES
TO HELP YOU THINK ABOUT THIS CHAPTER

Activity 1: It's time to get dirty in the data. Pick a brand that you use on a regular basis. Based on what's available through your school library, use at least three of the secondary resources described in this chapter to help you better understand the brand. What is at least one key insight from each resource you used?

Activity 2: Create a SWOT and SOAR analysis based on the information you've dug into for activity 1.

Activity 3: Using the information you've gathered in activities 1 and 2, imagine that this brand is going to be repositioned for a completely different target audience—someone more like your grandparents. Write a new SWOT or SOAR analysis for the brand.

REFERENCES

Experian. (n.d.). Connect the dots of consumer identity. Retrieved from https://www.experian.com/marketing-services/marketing-services.html

Statista. (n.d.a). About us. Retrieved from https://www.statista.com/aboutus

Statista. (n.d.b). Digital market outlook: Market directory. Retrieved from https://www.statista.com/outlook/digital-markets/market-directory

CHAPTER 7

Social Media Monitoring Tools

As you work through the chapters in the book, we hope you are beginning to better understand the depth of the relationship between a brand and its consumer. As you know by now, it is the responsibility of the account planner to observe the dynamics between the brand and the consumer in order to make this relationship even more engaging during the advertising campaign that you and your team are helping to develop. While there are all sorts of tools to enhance this relationship, social media is certainly one of the best.

This chapter will help you understand how to use social media to better understand your brands and your competitors' brands. It will also introduce you to free (or mostly free) monitoring tools that you can start using as a student. You'll learn how "listening" (or "monitoring") to social media chatter about your brands and your brand's competition will help you make connections to the other research you have been doing as you move toward developing an effective creative brief.

"Monitoring" has come under criticism recently. Many consumers have become increasingly concerned about privacy breaches. For example, a Time.com report (2018) explained the depth of the Cambridge Analytica Facebook hacking scandal affecting up to 87 million Facebook users. It's difficult to know for certain how far-reaching these hacking experiences are, but what it has done is bring privacy concerns to the forefront of many active social media users. Once it was discovered that commonly used sites like Facebook, Twitter, and even Google could be hacked, digitally focused companies have taken steps to increase security and also increase users' understanding of what they are "agreeing to" when they sign up for a particular service.

While it's true that we need to better understand our privacy rights and pay more attention to our social media footprints, ignoring social media as part of your advertising approach is simply not an option. Thinking back to chapter 2 and the explanation of the POEM (paid, owned, and earned media) model of advertising, social media is key to reaching and understanding your target audience, particularly when trying to increase "earned" media. As discussed previously, once we remember that ultimately the advertiser is really only interested in delivering appropriate content to the appropriate consumer, being able to better understand your brand's target audience with the advancement of analytics is an important ingredient in the advertising mix. It's no longer an *option* for better understanding your consumer. It's a *requirement*.

The challenge about monitoring social media feeds is trying to figure out how to uncover information that will be helpful to creating consumer insights without infringing on the privacy of specific individuals. One way to think of this is that although we create consumer personas as described in chapter 5, these are not actual people. They are representatives of the people you're trying to reach with your brand. Even so, you should treat these personas with respect, remembering that behind each consumer persona, there are many potential customers who want to connect with your brand. With that in mind, let's start monitoring social media.

We've already closely examined kinds of secondary research. In one way, social media monitoring is clearly secondary research, but it's so unique to other kinds of secondary research and so important to strategic advertising approaches that it warrants a separate chapter. So what is social media monitoring anyway? Paige Leidig (2018) broadly defines social media monitoring (the umbrella over all "listening" and "analytics") as "people sharing their lives with others they know—or get to know based on common interests." While she also argues that this isn't about brands per se, from an account planner's perspective, you can make it about brands. After all, once you begin to see that "brands" have personalities and that you're searching for innovative ways to connect the brand to the right target audience (also based on personalities), you aren't very far from Leidig's explanation of "people sharing their lives." In other words, you're conducting social media secondary research in order to figure out the appropriate ways for your brand to "share its life" with others ("consumers") who have a common interest with other consumers—and also with the brand. While it may sound a little bit "out there," building a brand personality requires the account planner to be willing to consider the brand as a kind of living, breathing individual—or at least a representative of an individual.

This isn't an exact science. The account planner needs to be creative and think of connections that others may have missed. If you remember that what you're really trying to do is understand connections in order to better understand both your consumer and your brand, you'll be better situated to jump in and think about this process proactively and creatively.

Companies engage in social media monitoring and listening for myriad reasons. What's important for you as a student considering a career in account planning is to make sure you understand you're "listening" to real people as well as company messages, and you have to respect your potential target audience's privacy as much as possible. As discussed previously, you need to make sure you're acting in an ethical manner in all your monitoring.

SOCIAL MEDIA SOURCES

Let's get started! Even if you don't think you've engaged in social media monitoring, you most likely already have. For example, have you ever conducted a Google search of yourself or of someone you wanted to know more about? That's a kind of monitoring. Likewise, checking out friends' Facebook pages and Twitter feeds are all a kind of social media monitoring. As an account planner, you'll still be interested in Google, Facebook, and Twitter, but you'll discover a lot of other tools as well that can help you strategically think about the brand you're representing. But let's start with the basics that you already know.

Google

"Monitoring" social media in its basic form is simply listening to the conversations happening on various social media platforms and then noticing patterns that might be helpful to your advertising strategy. Google, of course, is the logical place to start. Simply do a search of your brand. Try to think about the patterns that are emerging and then extend your search from there. Do you know who the competition is for your brand? (By now, you should have an idea.) Google the competition. If you've uncovered some research about your brand category, for example, and if there are articles in the research publications, you can go to Google Scholar and see what else is written by that researcher. You can also take a quick look at Google Images and see all sorts of pictures related to your brand. Once you've exhausted the "first run" with Google, you can move to the common social media sites that you're most likely already using regularly.

Twitter

As an example, let's think about the brand Vital Farms. Of course, the first step is to follow the brand. Vital Farms is found at @vitalfarms. You'll learn all sorts of information about the brand simply by following the company on Twitter. For example, you'll learn that Vital Farms isn't particularly active on Twitter, having only tweeted a handful of times over the last several months. For example, as of late 2018, Vital Farms had 4,306 followers and was following 567 others. The company has tweeted a total of 2,723 times since January 2011 when Vital Farms joined Twitter. While that isn't very active (for comparison purposes, Egglands Best eggs has more than 21,500 followers), this is still a treasure trove worth exploring. With just a keystroke, you have access to 567 people who are committed enough to Vital Farms that they follow the company on Twitter. Take a peek at some of the followers, and see if you can glean any insights that may be helpful for your advertising strategy.

However, that's only the beginning. Vital Farms is a company that sells pasture-raised eggs and ethically sourced butter. You should also follow the competition. But who is the competition to Vital Farms? Other pasture-raised egg producers, of course, such as Handsome Brook Farm and Backyard Eggs, are competitors. But perhaps you should also follow cage-free egg brands that aren't pasture raised as you try to understand how to situate your brand in the middle of a confusing ethical field.

Following brands on Twitter is only the beginning, of course. You should look at all the hashtags that your brand uses as well as hashtags that might be related to your brand. For example, Vital Farms uses the hashtag #girls ongrass, a reference to the egg-laying chickens (all girls, of course) and the pasture-fed concept. But others use the hashtag as well. And there are all sorts of similar hashtags such as #GrassFed and #RippingGrass. Clicking on these hashtags quickly uncovers other like-minded companies such as Green Pasture Farms and Dakota Grass Fed Beef. You can see that with just a few minutes on Twitter, you'll learn all sorts of helpful information that may be important to your advertising strategy development.

Facebook

Facebook, Instagram, and other social media sites that you might be using for your own enjoyment can yield helpful information for your brand. For example, for Facebook, simply "like" your brand's page and follow the newsfeed to see what information you might find. Continuing with the Vital Farms example, when you look at the company's page (remember, this is an example of "owned" media), you'll see beautiful photos of food and eggs (really, who knew that eggs could be so lovely?). You'll also see a post that explains about a recent egg recall, reassuring Vital Farms' customers that the recalled eggs aren't related to their eggs. From there, you'll find people's comments to the posts. You can click on their profile and learn information that might be helpful in discovering who the right target audience should be.

SOCIAL MEDIA MONITORING SITES

However, using Twitter, Facebook, and other popular social media sites is merely scratching the surface. The next step is to really dig in. Fortunately, there are several social media monitoring sites that can help you understand your brand and its consumers in a way that was nearly impossible even just a few years ago. Although many social media monitoring sites require a hefty subscription fee, others are completely free or have a free version available. As an account planning student, you'll gain lots of helpful skills and insights by using the free tools. Then, when you graduate and move to an agency, you'll be able to easily convert your skills to other more sophisticated monitoring tools that your agency may use. Following are some popular free (or free trial) social media monitoring tools that are available. Use these as a guide, but explore others on your own. With social media monitoring's lightning-speed growth, it's likely that there will be a whole host of new tools to try when you're ready to begin monitoring your brand.

Talkwalker

While you have to register to access the free version of the tool, it's a simple process. Once registered, simply type in your brand, and you'll quickly find all sorts of information that may be helpful to you. Doing a quick search of Vital Farms, you'll discover that the social media presence is primarily U.S. based (64.5%), followed by Canada (32.3%). You'll find that the sentiment for the brand is 58% positive and 4% negative with the rest categorized as neutral. This sentiment is for the time period examined, so it's important to check back regularly. For example, the second time running the analysis, the sentiment shows 39% positive and 3% negative, not too different from the original run, but this shows how quickly data can change. Talkwalker also allows you to view the time line of the engagement. In the case of these 3% negative comments, you'd notice that they all occurred around September 1. That's information that could be helpful as you research your brand.

When examining hashtags that Vital Farms uses, you'll get the data presented in a word cloud. Talkwalker also allows you to divide demographics. For example, if dividing the data by gender, you'll discover that on the day that the analysis was run, the top hashtag for women was #FoodTank.

Social Mention

Social Mention is another monitoring tool that is easy to use. You simply type the name of the brand you're investigating into the search feature on their website. In just a few moments you'll see percentages for four dimensions of your brand: strength, sentiment, passion, and reach. The "strength" dimension is the likelihood that the brand is being talked about on social media. The "sentiment" is the ratio of positive to negative mentions. The "passion" dimension measures the likelihood that someone who is talking about your brand will do it again. And "reach" is the ratio of unique mentions and total mentions. You also get other information on the page that reports these dimensions such as top keywords and top users. It's helpful to check out the top users as well. They can often lead you to some interesting insights that are beneficial to your brand.

While monitoring your brand's strength, passion, sentiment, and reach, it's important to monitor these numbers regularly since they can change. If they change drastically from one day to the next, for example, you can take a closer look and ascertain whether something happened that might be affecting your brand. If the strength, passion, sentiment, and reach are consistent over many days, that also is important information for you to use.

Social Mention does more than just get at the emotions of your brand in real time. It also indexes blogs, microblogs, bookmarks, images, videos, and questions people have asked online. After you type in the name of a brand, company, person, or whatever you're interested in and hit enter, you can sort the results by date or source in time frames ranging from the last hour to the last month. All the top social media platforms (and many more) are included in Social Mention's reports.

Boardreader

Boardreader goes out to a range of social media, including message boards, websites, and blogs, and then pulls posts that have the keyword (e.g., brand name) that you input. You can choose a date range to look at. Boardreader also has a function that lets you look at post activity graphically, using your choice of a line graph, bar chart, pie chart, or table. While Boardreader is free, you need to register to access more detailed information.

HowSociable

This free service tracks more than 250,000 brands. It provides a magnitude score, which shows how much activity a brand has had on social media in a specific week. Scores range from 0 to 10, with 10 indicating the greatest level of activity. The "pro" version of HowSociable looks across 36 websites, but you can get helpful data on one brand from 12 sites for free. While neither Facebook nor Instagram are included in the free sites, Tumblr, WordPress, Blogger, Reddit, YouTube, LinkedIn, and others are. Similar to many other free tools, you simply type in the name of the brand and wait for the results. If you use the free version of HowSociable, you're limited in the number of brands you can follow, but you can still garner a lot of information for your own brand.

Keyhole

Keyhole provides real-time monitoring of social media use as well as the ability to track historical information. For example, for its Facebook function, Keyhole will tell you the brand's average likes, comments, shares, engagement rate, and total page likes. It will give you a yearlong trend line on average and total engagements, likes, comments, and shares. You can see the top posts on the brand's page, ranked by engagement (likes, comments, and shares). Additionally, you'll get the optimal post length on the page to drive engagement, growth in followers, and the optimal times to post on the page based on time of day and day of the week. In the free-trial part of its website, Keyhole also works with Twitter, Instagram, and YouTube. Subscribers can get far more detailed information on a range of accounts, hashtags, and keywords at different price levels. Using Keyhole, for example, you discover that for the last week, Vital Farms had a peak activity on August 28. It may be worth investigating that day to see if there was any news that might be important to Vital Farms.

TweetReach

As you can guess from the name, TweetReach focuses on Twitter. You'll need to sign in with your Twitter handle, but then you can get a free snapshot for any brand that uses Twitter. The snapshot tells you the brand's estimated reach (number of Twitter accounts following the brand), exposure (impressions, broken down by users' numbers of followers), activity over a recent business day, top contributors, most retweeted Tweets, and recent Tweets. As with Keyhole, to make full use of TweetReach, you'll have to pay a fee, but you can try it out on their page. Continuing with Vital Farms, using TweetReach you'd discover that they have made 975,310 impressions with their most activity on August 28, 2018, which is consistent with Keyhole's analysis. With their organization of "contributors," you can quickly see who is most actively engaged with the brand, a helpful insight when trying to better understand both the brand and the consumer.

Hootsuite

Finally, Hootsuite is a popular monitoring tool for companies. It monitors Twitter, Facebook, LinkedIn, WordPress, and Foursquare for starters as well as allowing you to efficiently schedule tweets. While it's geared toward the paid audience, a 30-day free trial is available. There is also a limited free plan that offers the use of three profiles and one user. Hootsuite offers an extensive free student program that entire classes can use. And you can become certified in Hootsuite as part of the student program, which can be a valuable enhancement to your résumé as you begin your job search.

As you learn these different social media monitoring tools, it's important that you use multiple tools to get a deeper understanding of how your brand is performing. Even tools that monitor the same sites can yield different results. It's also important to remember that these examples of social media monitoring tools just scratch the surface of what is available. Don't limit yourself to these sites only. Instead, explore several others. You'll find that the more tools you use, the more you're able to understand how social media monitoring can work for uncovering successful customer and brand insights.

SUGGESTED ACTIVITIES
TO HELP YOU THINK ABOUT THIS CHAPTER

Activity 1: Pick a brand that you currently use. Check the brand's presence on Twitter. See how far you can go in learning about the brand. For example, how many hashtags are used that pertain to the brand? If you tweet about the brand, do you ever get a response from the brand? Check a couple of the brand's competitors. Which brand uses Twitter the best? Why do you think this?

Activity 2: Register for the free version of Talkwalker. Do a search for the brand you chose in activity 1, and view the time line of engagement. What new insights have you learned about the brand?

Activity 3: Use HowSociable's free service to check the brand you chose in activity 1 to see how much engagement the brand has had on social media in the last week. Do you think your brand is doing a good job engaging with its customers? Why or why not?

REFERENCES

Leidig, P. (2018, May 2). What is social media monitoring? Social media analytics guide. Netbase. Retrieved from https://www.netbase.com/blog/what-is-social-media-monitoring-sma-guide-part-2

Time.com. (2018, March 20). "Facebook's Cambridge Analytica controversy could be big trouble for the social network." http://time.com/5205314/facebook-cambridge-analytica-breach

CHAPTER 8

Primary Research

The Benefits and Pitfalls
of Quantitative Survey Research

As you might guess from our discussion of secondary research in chapter 6, primary research is research you conduct yourself, collecting new, timely information. There are a number of types of primary research, many of which we'll explore in this and the next chapter. But all primary research falls into one of two categories, quantitative studies and qualitative studies. Our focus in this chapter is on quantitative primary research, specifically on survey research.

Survey research, at its most basic level, is asking the same set of questions of a number of individuals. It can be a relatively quick way to gather a large amount of input to assist in various kinds of decision-making related to developing an advertising campaign. It's very important to be aware that surveys usually only help you figure out what's going on with a brand and product category; they won't necessarily tell you why things are occurring. But having quantitative, baseline information on what's going on with your brand and your target audience can be very helpful to the planner. In this chapter, we'll look at ways of conducting surveys, some of the types of questions survey data can help to answer, types of questions that can be asked, considerations in designing a survey, and some of the resources available to assist in survey development and administration.

WHY IS IT CALLED QUANTITATIVE?

Quantitative survey research involves asking a series of questions where the answers (or at least, most of them) can be converted into numerical data, which can then be analyzed using a variety of statistical techniques. Given the price tag of most advertising campaigns, many clients, understandably, are looking for some sense of certainty, and the "hard" answers provided by survey research can help with that.

But it's important to realize that surveys don't answer everything, and there are some definite concerns to keep in mind. First, the results of a survey are only as good as the survey itself. If you don't ask good questions, let alone the right questions to answer the problem you're trying to solve, getting thousands of responses to your survey won't be helpful. Second, a survey captures a snapshot in time; that is, it shows what people completing the survey were thinking, feeling, or doing at the time they took the survey. Their answers might be different a week from now than they were today. Third, the usefulness of a survey is also dependent on who takes the survey. If you're trying to solve a problem that deals with your target audience, you need to make sure that the people you ask to take the survey are in that target audience. (More on this in just a bit.) Finally, back to that sense of certainty. There are no absolute answers when you're dealing in questions that look at people's thoughts, feelings, and perceptions. You can get an indication of what's going on, but asking for 100% certainty is impossible.

USES FOR SURVEY RESEARCH

Surveys can be used to answer a wide range of questions, and there are thousands (maybe even hundreds of thousands) of surveys conducted in the United States every year. This can lead to respondent fatigue, so one of the most important rules in survey research is not to conduct a survey where you're asking questions about things that you can get answered elsewhere. Remember what we said about secondary research: No matter what, do secondary research first! You should only conduct a survey when there are questions you can't answer with secondary research.

What kinds of questions can a survey help an account planner answer? One major use for surveys is to discover the target audience's attitudes about the brand and its competitors as well as the expectations that audience has for the brand. A survey can also be used to gauge customer loyalty. How strongly do people feel about the brand? Why do those who buy it often choose to do so? Why are others not buying the brand as often?

Surveys can also be used to help flesh out the customer journey map by exploring where people are going to get information on the brand and what factors they consider when deciding which brand to buy. A survey can help identify patterns of product and service use, as with the Pew survey mentioned earlier. No matter what the particular focus may be, surveys are a useful tool for getting a snapshot of what's going on with a large number of people.

SAMPLING

As previously discussed, you want to make sure you're administering your carefully designed survey to the right people. To do that, the first step is to define the population you're interested in. The population is the larger group you want to study. If you think back to our earlier target market description in chapter 5, the population would be all women aged 35–44 living in the Northeast with kids aged 13–16 at home. If you can truly get a definitive list of everyone who fits those characteristics, that would be a census. But that's not really possible, so instead, you consider people you *can* identify to be part of that population. But you're not going to ask all of them to complete your survey because that would cost too much money and likely take too long. Plus, you don't need all of them to take your survey to get useful information. Instead, you can choose a sample from the population.

How many people do you need to talk to? To answer that question, you need to determine what the acceptable confidence level is for your study. What does that mean? The confidence level is the likelihood that if you surveyed a different group of people from the same population, you'd get the same results. A 99% confidence level means you'd get the same results 99 times out of 100. A 95% confidence level means you'd get the same results 95 times out of 100, and so on. The way you get to a higher confidence level is by surveying more people, because the sample size needed to reach a particular confidence level is proportional to the size of the overall population.

Desired confidence level is one element in sample size. The margin of error you (and your client) are comfortable with is another. When you're dealing with a sample instead of the entire population, there is a statistical assumption that the results from that sample won't be exactly what you would find if you really did survey everyone in the population. Common acceptable margins of error (the +/– difference in what you found in the sample versus what would probably be the case if you'd surveyed the entire population) are 5%, 2.5%, and 1%. As with confidence level, the larger the sample relative to the population, the lower the margin of error.

So, let's say we're interested in surveying members of a target audience that has a population size of 10,000 people. To attain a 95% confidence level with a 2.5% margin of error, we'd need to survey 1,332 people. To attain a 99% confidence level with that same 2.5% margin of error, we'd need to survey 2,098 people. See how it works?

Here's a practical example. The Pew Research Center released a study in August 2018 that looked at how U.S. parents and teenagers use their mobile devices (Jiang, 2018). The researchers surveyed 1,058 parents of teenagers and 743 teenagers (all of them children of surveyed parents). At the 95% confidence level, the margin of error for the parents was 4.5%; for the teens, the margin of error was 5%. For the results of some of the questions, the researchers subdivided the teens by gender and age. Because each of those subdivisions was a smaller group of survey respondents relative to the overall population of U.S. teens, the margin of error goes up. For example, the margin of error for teens between the ages of 13 and 14, still at the 95% confidence level, was 7.8%.

Now that you have an idea of how large a sample you'll need to get the statistical precision you want, how do you draw that sample? The gold standard in sampling is the simple random sample. In a simple random sample, every person in the population has an equal likelihood of being selected to participate.

It may be called "simple," and it may sound simple, but it's not. Unless you're dealing with a small, tightly defined population—all of whom you can identify and reach—it's impossible to draw a simple random sample. Instead, we do the best we can and rely on confidence levels and margins of error to help us know how reliable the data are.

The Pew study is a good example of the challenge of random samples. Pew is a highly regarded research organization. Rather than using a simple random sample to select the parents and teens who were asked to complete the survey on mobile device use, they drew their sample from an existing consumer panel developed by NORC (formerly called National Opinion Research Center) at the University of Chicago, a nonpartisan and objective research organization. NORC operates an AmeriSpeak panel. AmeriSpeak is "a nationally representative, probability-based panel of the U.S. household population." What does *that* mean?

You can read a detailed description of how the AmeriSpeak panel is constructed on the AmeriSpeak website (AmeriSpeak, n.d.). Basically, the panel is designed to map onto the overall U.S. population primarily in terms of geography, and then oversampled to ensure there are households included with younger people and with good representation of minority households. It's that oversampling (i.e., including more households of a specific type) that prevents this from being a simple random sample.

To circle back to our initial discussion, what matters most for an account planner is that you're surveying people in the brand's target market and, ideally, in that more detailed target audience. It's important to think about how you'll find those people and how you'll select the people you include. But don't get frustrated trying to draw a simple random sample because the reality is, you can't. Instead, be able to explain what you did to get your survey respondents, and be able to support why what you did was appropriate. The primary question you need to be able to answer is, what larger population is your sample representative of?

SCREENER QUESTIONS

From the previous discussion, it should be clear that you want to make sure you're surveying the right people, people who are in your target population. One way to do that is to start by asking screener questions. Screener questions are ones that qualify people for participation in your survey.

Some screener questions may ask about demographics, as in the case where you're trying to get responses from people across an age group. Screener questions often deal with product usage, either current or past use of a particular product category or even of a specific brand within that category. Deciding whether you need to use screener questions and, if so, what they should be is an important initial step in developing your survey.

TYPES OF QUESTIONS

Once you've set your screener questions, it's time to move into the meat of the survey. Just as there are many possible purposes for a survey, there are a number of ways of asking questions. The discussion that follows is by no means all-inclusive, but it looks at some widely used types of questions. We've also given an example for each type of question, all around the brand we looked at in chapter 5, Honey Nut Cheerios.

Likert Statements

Creating Likert statements is a common way of asking questions about attitudes. A scale with an odd number of answer choices (usually five but sometimes more) is used, and the respondents select the choice that most closely matches their feelings. The scale assumes there is an equal distance between each of the options. Here is an example:

Honey Nut Cheerios is a healthy breakfast cereal.

Strongly disagree	Disagree	Neither agree nor disagree	Agree	Strongly agree

Semantic Differentials

In a semantic differential statement, the survey respondents are given pairs of opposite words and then asked to indicate along a scale (again, usually one with an odd number of options) which of the two words aligns most closely with their feelings.

I think Honey Nut Cheerios is

Healthy		———	———	———	———		Unhealthy
Delicious		———	———	———	———		Bad tasting
For kids		———	———	———	———		For adults

Multiple Choice

In a multiple-choice question, the respondents are given a range of answer options and asked to pick the one (or several) that best matches their feelings. How many answer options you allow the respondent to choose depends on your objective in asking the question. Here are two examples, one where the respondents can choose as many statements that apply and one where they have to make one choice.

People who eat Honey Nut Cheerios are (choose all that apply)
——— Mothers
——— Fathers
——— Little kids
——— Teenagers
——— Young adults
——— Senior citizens

The main reason people eat Honey Nut Cheerios is that they like (choose one)
——— The honey taste
——— The nuts
——— The cost
——— The health aspects
——— The bee character

Rating Scale

In a rating scale question, respondents are asked to evaluate particular products or characteristics on a set scale where the answer options are each equally distant.

Please rate the sweetness of Honey Nut Cheerios on a scale of 1 to 10, where 1 means not sweet at all and 10 means extremely sweet.

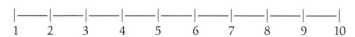

|———|———|———|———|———|———|———|———|———|
1   2   3   4   5   6   7   8   9   10

Ranking

In a ranking question, respondents are given a list of related items and asked to rank order them according to the directions from the researcher. Here is an example of a ranking question.

Please rank the following brands of breakfast cereal from 1 to 5 based on how sweet you believe them to be. Rank the brand you consider to be the sweetest 1, the brand you consider to be the second sweetest 2, and so on.
—— Apple Jacks
—— Cinnamon Toast Crunch
—— Frosted Mini-Wheats
—— Golden Grahams
—— Honey Nut Cheerios

Open-Ended versus Closed-Ended Questions

All the question types above are examples of closed-ended questions—that is, questions where the survey respondent's only choices for answers are those that we've given them. Some surveys also include open-ended questions, where the respondents are free to answer whatever they wish. If you were surveying Honey Nut Cheerios users, you could simply ask, "What do you like best about Honey Nut Cheerios?" On the helpful side, you'd probably get a wide range of answers, and some of them might tell you things about Honey Nut Cheerios you hadn't thought about. On the not-so-helpful side, answers to open-ended questions are more time consuming to interpret and can't be analyzed using statistical methods. However, if you're not sure you know all the possible answers your respondents might want to choose from, or you're looking for undiscovered insights, open-ended questions are a good option. (An even better option is to use a qualitative research method. Those are discussed in the next chapter.)

Choosing Question Types

What type of question should you use? Obviously, it depends on what you're trying to find out. But whatever you're trying to discover, the results will only be as good as the question itself. So think about your question choices in terms of the people who will be taking your survey. If you're going to screen for people who are current users of Honey Nut Cheerios or have eaten them in the past, you'll want to ask different types questions than if you were going to survey people who don't eat breakfast cereal.

For example, the ranking and rating questions above might work well with the current/past users group, because they'd have a reasonable frame of reference for it. But it wouldn't work too well with nonusers. But both a current/past user and a nonuser could probably answer the other types of questions based on either their knowledge (current/past user) or their perceptions (nonuser).

SOME COMMON CHALLENGES
FOR DEVELOPING SURVEY QUESTIONS

While there are many ways to ask questions, there are some ways you need to avoid. There are several types of problematic questions that will not only confuse your survey respondents but also frustrate you when it comes time to analyze your survey results.

Double-Barreled Questions

A double-barreled question asks about two different ideas within the same question. If the respondent's answer to each of the two things isn't the same, but you're forcing them into one answer, that answer isn't going to be helpful. In the question below, what if the person is allergic to nuts but likes the idea of whole grain? The nut allergy would probably take the lead and they'd answer "very unlikely," but you wouldn't know that whole grain is appealing.

How likely would you be to eat a breakfast cereal that has nuts in it and is made with whole grain?
———— Very likely
———— Likely
———— Neither likely nor unlikely
———— Unlikely
———— Very unlikely

Leading Questions

A leading question is one that is written in such a way that the survey designer is already suggesting the direction of the answer. You're conducting a survey to find out what your survey respondents think, not to simply reinforce your own beliefs. The question below is leading in two ways: the wording of the question itself, because it's asking how strongly the respondents agree, not whether they agree or not, and in the answer choices, because there are no degrees of disagreement given as options.

How strongly do you agree that whole grain is a very important aspect of a healthy breakfast cereal?
—— Very strongly agree
—— Strongly agree
—— Agree
—— Neither agree nor disagree
—— Disagree

Loaded Questions

A loaded question pushes the respondent to answer in a certain way, usually by implying something that may not actually be the case. In the question below, respondents would probably be reluctant to choose an answer that indicates they don't eat cereal very often, because the question suggests that smart people *do* eat cereal.

People who are concerned about their health know that breakfast is the most important meal of the day, and healthy cereals are an important part of a healthy breakfast. How often do you eat cereal for breakfast?
—— All of the time
—— Most of the time
—— Some of the time
—— Every once in a while
—— Never

Absolute Questions

An absolute question forces the respondent into making a choice that might not really reflect what they do or don't believe. In the question below, what if the person would actually prefer to have yogurt for breakfast at home? You won't learn that from this question.

Would you rather have cereal for breakfast at home or eat breakfast at a restaurant?
—— Eat cereal at home
—— Eat at a restaurant

Other Question Considerations

When you're asking people about past behavior, it's important to give them a specific time frame, both to aid in their recollection and so that you know you're comparing the same time frame across respondents. And with any question involving actions in the past, it's important to make sure that the time frame is realistic. For example, it's fine to ask people how many times in the last seven days, or two weeks, or month they ate Honey Nut Cheerios for breakfast. But asking them how often they ate Honey Nut Cheerios in the last six months is more problematic. That's something close to 180 different breakfasts, and it's not likely anyone would remember that accurately. If you're trying to estimate usage in a six-month time frame, it's better to ask about the past month and then just multiply by six.

Another problem is the use of double negatives, which serve to confuse (and possibly irritate) your respondents. Here's a question with a double negative: "Which of the following aspects of Honey Nut Cheerios do you not find unappealing?" Do you want to know what people like about Honey Nut Cheerios, or what they don't like? Your respondents would have to give some thought to sorting out this question, and chances are some people will answer one way (choosing things they find unappealing) while others will take the opposite view (choosing things they find appealing). That would leave you with responses that are difficult to interpret and even misleading.

Also, try to avoid using unfamiliar jargon or acronyms. While you may be an expert on the brand, the category, and advertising, your respondents aren't. Keep your questions simple for the best results. By "best results" we mean collecting usable surveys, where your respondents have answered all the questions, and because the questions were written clearly, the results will be truly useful.

Design Considerations

When you put your survey together, it's also necessary to think about question order. Start with any needed screener questions, then move to general questions (such as asking about product category use), and then to specific questions (such as questions about the brand). Unless you needed them for screeners, put all questions about demographic characteristics (e.g., age, income, and marital status) at the end of the survey. Not everyone likes to answer those types of questions. But if you put them at the end, after the respondents have already invested time in answering your other questions, they're more likely to go ahead and answer the demographics as well.

FIELDING YOUR SURVEY

There are a few other issues to look at in survey research. One basic question, which you'll probably answer before you start to compose the survey, is how you'll distribute it to respondents. There are several options, including telephone surveys, mail surveys, face-to-face surveys (either door-to-door or intercepting people at shopping centers or other gathering sites), and online surveys. Each option has significant drawbacks as well as benefits, but online surveys are being used more and more for reasons of cost, convenience, and speed of data collection. Businesses are also experimenting with conducting surveys through social media, but one of the big concerns there is the lack of ability to control who has access to the survey. Getting a lot of survey responses doesn't matter if most of them are from people outside the target population.

There are a number of useful online survey sites that offer tools to help you design your survey and that will also tabulate results for you. Three that are widely used are Qualtrics (https://www.qualtrics.com), SurveyMonkey (https://www.surveymonkey.com) and MTurk (https://www.mturk.com). Many universities subscribe to at least one of these survey sites, so check to see what might be available that you can use for free while you're a student.

FINAL CONSIDERATIONS

A key rule in any type of primary research is to be respectful of your respondents. You're asking people to give up their time to answer your questions, and depending on what it is that you're asking, you might also be expecting them to share personal information. No matter what method you're using to share your survey, you need to give people an idea of how much time it will take them to complete the survey—and that estimate needs to be accurate. Telling someone you need "just 5 minutes of your time" for a survey that will actually take 20 minutes not only is unethical but will also lead to many people abandoning the survey partway through.

Another way to be respectful of people's time is to only ask questions seeking information that you can't find elsewhere. (Remember: Always do secondary research first!) You want to make your survey as efficient as possible. Yes, you want to gather the needed information to meet the objectives you began with, but don't pad the survey with unnecessary questions that aren't relevant to your objectives.

To avoid as many of the possible problems described in this chapter as possible, always, *always* test your survey before fielding it. Ask people who weren't involved in the survey's creation—and who aren't experts on the brand—to take the survey, and then debrief them afterward. Were there questions they didn't understand? Things that were confusing? Questions that took a long time to answer? And how long did it take them to complete the survey? You want to make sure that the survey you put out in the field is in the best shape possible.

What if you didn't design the survey but you're looking at survey results to aid in developing the creative brief? First, start by reviewing the survey methodology. Any good research report will include a thorough discussion of how the sampling was done, how the survey was fielded, and similar information. That discussion is also where you'll find the confidence level and margin of error. Then, read through the actual questions that were asked and the answer options respondents were given. If at all possible, do this before you begin to look at the results. At the very least, go back to the original question for any results you find puzzling.

Finally, always remember that surveys can be a useful quantitative tool, but they only tell you "what," not "why." While they can be a starting point for unlocking insights, they won't always get you to that breakthrough idea. Qualitative research methods tend to deal more in the "why." That's what we'll look at in the next chapter.

SUGGESTED ACTIVITIES
TO HELP YOU THINK ABOUT THIS CHAPTER

Activity 1: Let's say you want to go on a road trip with five of your friends. "Your friends" is your target market. Make a list of 25 friends, and ask each of them this screener question: "Do you like to take long road trips by car?" (You may want to define "long" as part of your survey.)

Activity 2: Write the names of those who said yes to your first question on small pieces of paper. Let's say that you get 12 who would like to go on a road trip with you, but you only have room for four people and yourself in your car. Fold these up and put them in a bowl. Randomly select four names from the bowl. This is your random sample.

Activity 3: Develop a survey of three questions. For example, let's say you want to know where your friends would like to take a road trip, and you might ask them that open-ended question. Let's say you get five similar responses from your friends. Take those responses, and ask each of your five friends to rank order where they would want to go from (1) the place they would most want to go to (5) the place they would least want to go. You could then figure out which place your group would most want to go on your road trip. And happy travels!

REFERENCES

AmeriSpeak. (n.d.). Panel design. Retrieved from https://amerispeak.norc.org /Documents/Research/AmeriSpeak%20Technical%20Overview%202019%20 02%2018.pdf

Jiang, J. (2018, August 22). How teens and parents navigate screen time and device distractions. Pew Research Center. Retrieved from http://www.pewinternet .org/2018/08/22/how-teens-and-parents-navigate-screen-time-and-device-distrac tions

CHAPTER 9

Primary Research

Qualitative, Consumer Style

As we saw in the last chapter, quantitative survey research generates data that can be projected to a larger population. Not only do we learn what the particular people surveyed are thinking, feeling, and doing, but also we have some confidence that those people's responses are representative of the larger group we selected them to represent.

With qualitative research, we try to peer into the so-called black box, the brain, including the subconscious. Where a quantitative survey can answer the question of "what," qualitative methods help us get to the "why."

While account planners certainly work with survey research data quite often, many swear by qualitative research as the workhorse in helping to uncover insights. In this chapter we'll look at some of the major types of qualitative research, including focus groups, ethnography, and depth interviews, among others.

FOCUS GROUPS

Focus groups are a commonly used advertising research tool. Focus groups play off of socialization and group dynamics, generating discussion on a particular topic among a group of people who have something in common. Most often, what they have in common is category or brand usage, but you might also compose a group of a particular demographic or psychographic characteristic. For Honey Nut Cheerios, for example, you might conduct focus groups among working moms who have kids in a particular age range.

You want to get a discussion going among the group regarding the questions you're interested in answering. Where a depth interview (see below) lets you get into a detailed conversation with an individual, focus groups focus on the group dynamics and the conversation around the table. Focus groups can be used to explore a range of issues, both early on while you're looking for an insight and then later when you're testing advertising concepts. Often, the most useful information from a focus group comes through the discussion among the group participants as they talk among themselves about their reactions to issues brought up by the focus group moderator.

If you're considering using focus groups, start by looking at the questions you want to answer and the objectives for the research and whether those can best be met through focus groups. For example, let's imagine you're trying to get a better sense of what the weekday breakfast time is like for working moms. You could interview moms individually, but hearing the conversation among a group of moms as they compare notes and share their frustrations will likely give you much deeper insight into this part of their day. So, a focus group would be a good means of getting at that information.

Once you've determined that focus groups are indeed an appropriate method in your situation, the next step is to identify an experienced focus group moderator. You'll work with that person on the desired flow of the focus group and the particular questions that will be asked. (The list of questions is called a moderator's guide.) As with a survey, you want to move from more general questions to more specific questions. So in our example, you'd start by having the moms introduce themselves and talk a little about their families and then move into a general conversation about family mealtimes. From there, you would move to talking about breakfast specifically and what's different about weekday versus weekend breakfast. Next, you might move the discussion to talking about breakfast foods, then to cereal specifically, and then to brands. As your focus group participants get more comfortable with one another, and with the moderator, the conversation generally gets richer and deeper.

Generally, the focus group discussion is recorded and also captured on video (with the participants' advance agreement, of course). While the moderator takes notes during the focus group, other interested parties, including the account planner, may be observing unobtrusively. Having the recording of the focus group makes it possible to go back to the discussion multiple times, looking for nuances like body language, facial expressions, and tone of voice that might have been missed initially. It's often those nuanced things that point to what's truly important to your focus group participants, and that might get you to the heart of the strategy. Being able to refer to the recordings, or transcripts of them, will also give you time to look for patterns and themes in the discussion.

As with surveys, focus group participants should be chosen because they're part of the target audience. It's common to provide refreshments during the focus group (the goal is for people to feel comfortable), and focus group participants are often paid for their time or given some other form of compensation.

Focus groups are usually conducted in person to better facilitate the flow of the conversation, but they are sometimes done over the telephone or online. Which approach makes the most sense depends on how much time you have to conduct the groups and your budget, and also the nature of the participants themselves. For example, if you want to conduct focus groups among teenagers, and the topic is something where peer pressure might be a concern, the relative anonymity of a telephone focus group might make sense.

How many focus groups do you need to conduct? More than one is ideal, but usually somewhere around three to four groups will be sufficient to draw some inferences about the question at hand. When you start to hear similar comments and observations between the different groups, then you'll know that you've probably gathered enough input and don't need to do any additional focus groups.

ETHNOGRAPHY

Many account planners are particularly fond of ethnography as a research tool. Ethnography comes out of anthropology; it involves taking a deep look into people's lives and culture. Think about researchers such as Margaret Mead, a cultural anthropologist, living among their subjects to closely observe their daily lives and practices. In ethnographic advertising research, we're trying to do something similar to understand as much as possible about how our product or service fits into the target audience's life. Sure, you can ask questions through a survey or even in a focus group to discover the interaction between your target audience and your brand, but actually seeing that interaction can be much more revealing than anything someone might be able to tell you.

When UNIQLO was getting ready to launch its first stores in Toronto, Canada, they worked with their agency, Leo Burnett Toronto, to understand what would motivate consumers in the city. Other retailers had tried and failed to establish their brands in Toronto, and UNIQLO wanted to be a success story. As part of the research they conducted before the launch, they used ethnography to talk with a wide range of Toronto residents in neighborhoods throughout the city. The focus in this research was less about retailing and more about overall lifestyle and what people liked most and least about living in Toronto. While UNIQLO also used some other types of qualitative research in developing their introductory campaign, the ethnographic research was a critical component. The resulting campaign, #UncommonThread, won a 2018 ARF David Ogilvy Award for its use of research (ARF, 2018).

The CIA (Consumer Insights Agency, http://www.the-cia.co.za), based in Cape Town, South Africa, is a research company that works for clients in multiple countries across several continents. The CIA specializes in ethnographic research, and its team of interviewer/observers, with unobtrusive recorders in hand (previously very small handheld video recorders, today more often microphone-enhanced smartphones), talk to people living in all types of settings about the products they use and the lives they lead. The CIA is a big believer in letting consumers speak for themselves; in presenting their findings to clients, they rely on their own observations, trend analysis, and semiotics, as well as on videos their team has collected, so clients can see for themselves how consumers are using, and talking about, their brand. The CIA's mantra is, "A desk is a dangerous place from which to view the world," and that's a good description of the power of ethnography.

That power can be seen in work the CIA did for Johnson & Johnson's baby products division. The client wanted to get a sense of how mothers of young children felt about the process of washing their children's hair and the various products involved. The CIA's field team spent time with moms and kids in their homes, first listening to the moms talk about the process and then being there as the moms washed their children's hair. The challenges and frustrations (for both the mom and the child) come through very strongly in the videos from the sessions and really helped everyone understand where the pressure points were and how products from Johnson & Johnson might make the process less stressful.

When does it make the most sense to use ethnography? Evok Advertising is a Florida-based agency group that specializes in social media work and relies heavily on ethnography. They believe ethnography is particularly helpful when you're launching a new product or working to relaunch an existing product, developing a brand position, or just trying to get a better understanding of how consumers use the brand in their everyday lives (https://www.evokad.com). Imagine using ethnography with our Honey Nut Cheerios families, hanging out with them in their homes during breakfast time, seeing what goes on. What a great way to really understand family dynamics and just how breakfast works in a busy household.

NETNOGRAPHY

Netnography is a relatively new adaptation of ethnography to the world of social media. The term was developed by Robert V. Kozinets, who holds an endowed chair in public relations at the University of Southern California. Netnography involves looking at exchanges and conversations on social media to understand people's thinking and behavior. It's certainly related to ethnography, but as a method, netnography has a specific set of guidelines for how it should be conducted and how the findings should be analyzed and interpreted. It's social media monitoring following a specific process.

Netnography uses data collected online, particularly in social media forums, but also uses interviews with individuals to provide context for the online communications. The netnographic researcher also keeps careful field notes as they're observing the ongoing discussions (Netnography, n.d.). Given the range of opinions and information many people are willing to share on social media, this is a qualitative research tool that's likely to grow in importance among advertising researchers.

DEPTH INTERVIEWS

Depth interviews are one-on-one, detailed conversations between a researcher and a consumer respondent. While the format of question and answer may sound like a survey, the questions in a depth interview are always open ended, and the answer to one question can lead to multiple, increasingly detailed follow-up questions.

The vitamin supplement brand Emergen-C used depth interviews as part of a research study to figure out how to reposition the brand from a wintertime anticold supplement to a year-round wellness product. The researchers used projective techniques (see below) to explore how people who were already using Emergen-C throughout the year felt about the brand. They learned that regular users are often in situations where they feel stressed and vulnerable. They saw Emergen-C as something that helped them take control of at least one aspect of their lives. The research behind the creative advertising campaign developed from this insight, "Emerge & See," won Pfizer Consumer Healthcare, the maker of Emergen-C, and its agencies, Grey Advertising, Revolution Digital, and Tracey Locke, a 2018 ARF David Ogilvy Award (ARF, 2018).

As always, the account planner needs to think carefully about the objective of the research and whether depth interviews are the best choice. In the case of Emergen-C, the researchers found initially that regular users had trouble explaining why they were using Emergen-C routinely. The deeper probing possible with a depth interview was the best way to get at the underlying motivations.

CUSTOMER INTERCEPTS

In customer intercepts, the researcher is seeking to talk to people in the target audience at or close to the point of purchase. As we mentioned at the outset of this chapter, one of the strengths of qualitative research is being able to get at the "why," and talking to people just after they've made a brand choice can be helpful in exploring why they just chose the brand they did. The decision is fresh in their minds, and they're right there with the brand in their hand or shopping basket. (Important caveat: Get permission from the store owner or manager first!)

As with all other types of research, you need to first think carefully about the type of person you want to interview and why they'll be helpful in what you're trying to explore. You could easily station yourself in the cereal aisle in the supermarket and see who picks up Honey Nut Cheerios or one of its main competitors, but you don't necessarily want to talk to every person who makes that brand choice. If we stay with our focus on moms, you wouldn't want to interview males, or people who look as if they're probably single. So, you need to think through what kind of people you want to interview and then determine some parameters for whom you will or won't approach to request a conversation.

Researchers need to always be respectful of their respondents' time and privacy, and the time consideration is particularly important with customer intercepts. You're interrupting this person's shopping, and if they agree to talk with you in the first place, you'll need to keep it short and focused. This means question choice is paramount. You want to get to the heart of what you're interested in quickly, gather the information you need, and then let the person go. It's also common to offer an incentive as a thank you, such as a coupon or something similar. (But do that after the interview, not before, so the answers won't be biased.)

For Honey Nut Cheerios, you might approach a mom-looking person right after she's picked a box up off the shelf and put it in her cart. You'd introduce yourself, explain that you're conducting a research study on breakfast cereal (*not* the brand), tell her about how long the interview should take, and ask if she's willing to participate. If she says yes, you'd then start with your questions. The conversation might go something like this: "I see you just picked up a box of Honey Nut Cheerios. Have you eaten those before?" If she says yes, "What do you like about Honey Nut Cheerios?" If she says no, "Why did you decide to try them now?" Then, in either case, "Who in your family eats the Honey Nut Cheerios?" Depending on that answer, you could probe a little further based on who is or isn't eating them. You could wrap up by asking, "Is there anything else you'd like to tell me about Honey Nut Cheerios or about breakfast cereal in general?" And then finish by thanking her for her time and giving her a coupon.

That may sound simple, and you may wonder how helpful such a short interview can be. But hearing the words people use in talking about the brand, even seeing how interested they are (or aren't) in discussing it can help you get a much better idea of how important the brand is, or isn't, in their lives. Customer intercepts aren't always the right method, but they can be very helpful when you're focusing on why people select one brand over others. Again, it's that opportunity to talk with them immediately after they've made their brand choice while the decision is fresh in their minds that is most helpful.

PROJECTIVE TECHNIQUES

Projective techniques are not a qualitative research methodology in themselves, but they are tools that can be used as part of a variety of qualitative methods, including in focus groups and depth interviews. The goal behind projective techniques is to discover underlying motivations that the respondent may not be consciously aware of. Below are some commonly used projective techniques.

Word association. You've probably played games like this before, but word association can provide interesting insights. In this technique, the researcher develops a list of words or terms related to the product category, brand, or usage situation. The respondents are asked to say the first thing that comes to their mind when they hear that word or phrase. For Honey Nut Cheerios, prompt words could be things such as *breakfast, cereal, honey,* and so on. The emphasis on replying with the first thing that comes to mind is intended to get at what's most quickly accessed in the consumer's black box instead of spending some time trying to come up with the answer the respondent thinks the researcher wants to hear.

Sentence completion. Here, the researcher starts a sentence and asks the respondent to complete it, again saying whatever comes to mind first. "People who eat cereal for breakfast are . . ."; "Healthy breakfast cereals taste . . ."; and so on. There's a little more contextual guidance with sentence completion than with word association, but the underlying principle is the same.

Image association. This is similar to word association, but the prompts are pictures rather than words. Here, the researcher might show the respondent a picture of a bowl of cereal, of a field of ripening grain, or of a honeybee on a flower. What kind of response does each picture evoke?

Cartoon captions. As with image association, the stimulus here is visual, but in this case it's a cartoon frame or frames, and the respondent supplies the caption to explain what's going on. You could develop a cartoon of a frazzled mom in a kitchen with kids milling about and various breakfast items on the counter and then see how your mom respondents would caption it.

Collage construction. Another visually based projective technique, in collage construction respondents are given a range of images, fabric swatches, color chips, or any kind of visual items and are then asked to create a collage that represents how they feel about something of interest to the researcher. It could be a collage on how having to get breakfast into the kids every morning makes you feel, or of what images come to mind when you think of Honey Nut Cheerios.

Storytelling. This can be a richly revealing projective technique. Storytelling is something of an elaboration on sentence completion, but instead of just finishing a sentence, the respondent develops a story from a prompt provided by the researcher. The prompt can be the opening sentences of a story, a situation, or a visual—really anything that will cue a story.

ANALYSIS AND USE OF QUALITATIVE FINDINGS

As you've probably realized by now, one of the primary challenges of using qualitative research is interpreting the results. It's not cut-and-dried like a survey. You're not reporting how many people chose answer A versus B versus C. Instead, you're looking across responses to the same prompt to find *patterns* that can lead you to an insight. Every once in a while, the insight is obvious. However, much of the time, it takes real immersion into the results, reading focus group transcripts repeatedly or watching ethnographic videos over and over. But you'll be pleasantly surprised by how often qualitative methods do yield rich, useful insights, as in the Emergen-C example mentioned earlier.

Looking at the process the CIA research agency uses might help you better understand how qualitative research can be implemented and then analyzed. It starts when they get a brief from the client, the assignment of what the client is hoping to learn/uncover. A very important next step is to clarify their own assumptions as well as those of the client, so that everyone is clear on what potential biases they're bringing into the discovery process. Next, the CIA determines who the client's consumer is and then discovers the worldview, mind set, and experiences of those consumers. What really matters to them? From that deep consumer understanding, they can then begin to figure out what the role of the brand is (or isn't) in the consumer's world. What the CIA is looking for is the human truths around the consumer's life and the brand that will lead to an insight. The CIA has a structured approach but also recognizes that the consumer's world is very fluid; they're thinking in terms of strategy and insights from their first interview with or observation of someone in the client's target audience.

The debate aspect of the inspired insight stage is particularly important. There are no certainties in qualitative research (in quantitative too for that matter); everything is open to interpretation; that's part of the reason that recognizing assumptions from the beginning is so important. But it's informed interpretation that emerges from the time the CIA's field researchers have spent in their observations and conversations, and the hours the team has spent reviewing video, listening to what consumers have to say. They'll also test the deductions they've made from their time in the field with the consumers themselves, to make sure they're truly representing the consumer's view, not the researcher's. It's critical that the account planner eats, sleeps, and breathes how the customer feels about the brand, because it's that passion that will lead to the insight, and it's the confidence the planner has in that insight that will need to be communicated to the client to convince the client that this is the right strategy for the brand.

A final thought: one of the biggest challenges for an account planner in using qualitative methods can be convincing the client that insights developed in this way are legitimate. Many clients "get it" (and the more highly successful advertising campaigns there are that have emerged from qualitative studies, the easier the convincing becomes), but some will want to have numbers. How many people were in the focus groups? How many depth interviews did you conduct? So, be prepared to be asked and to be able to answer those kinds of questions. But your emphasis in presenting results and making recommendations based on those results should be on the power of the insight—and trying to help your clients better understand the people who are buying their product (or who they wish were buying it).

With this review of some of the kinds of secondary and primary research account planners use most often, you have the basic tools. Now, let's look at account planning in action, starting with looking more deeply into how strategies are revealed through the advertising they inspire.

SUGGESTED ACTIVITIES
TO HELP YOU THINK ABOUT THIS CHAPTER

Activity 1: As we discussed in chapter 6, researchers should always start with secondary research before moving on to primary research, whether quantitative or qualitative. For this activity, approach your travel question from a qualitative perspective. You've selected your four travel buddies. Now you want to decide where to go. Rather than asking quantitative questions, take a qualitative approach. Imagine that you are going to host a focus group of your friends. Make a list of some of the questions you might ask them. Explain why these would be good questions for a focus group.

Activity 2: Rather than a focus group, for this activity think about depth interviews with your friends. What questions would you ask them? Compare these questions to the focus group questions. How are they different?

Activity 3: Explore your friends' interests with projective techniques. Let's say you have three options you want to hone in on—Yosemite National Park in California, Yellowstone National Park in Wyoming, and the Grand Canyon in Arizona. How could you explore these options with projective techniques? Explain at least three different approaches you could take.

REFERENCES

ARF (Advertising Research Foundation). (2018). The ARF David Ogilvy Awards at Consumer Science 2018: Winners. Retrieved from https://thearf.org/2018-arf-david-ogilvy-awards-winners

Netnography. (n.d.). In *Wikipedia*. Retrieved from https://en.wikipedia.org/wiki/Netnography

CHAPTER 10

Unwrapping Advertising Strategy by Working Backward

A Helpful Exercise for Account Planners

Examining an advertisement and "working backward" to determine the target audience, the advertising strategy, and tone, as well as the key consumer insight, is an important skill for any student interested in account planning. Therefore, this chapter will help you better understand how to interpret advertising from an account planner's perspective.

While account planners may not produce the creative execution behind the actual advertising campaign, they are laying the groundwork that will enable the creative team to take over and finish the job. For advertising students hoping to become account planners, it's critical to understand the process of researching the brand, the brand's competition, and the brand's potential consumers. But you can't stop there. You also have to deeply understand the *advertising strategy* that will yield a successful campaign. This skill doesn't come naturally. It takes work to learn how to develop appropriate advertising strategies that allow the planner to zero in on the appropriate target audience. In other words, if you're going to be a planner, you need to deeply understand the advertising strategy behind the message. Once you understand more fully how important advertising strategy is to building a strong campaign, you'll be able to continue to develop your strategy skills. That way, you'll be able not only to develop a strong strategy yourself but also to communicate it to others. The first step, however, is understanding what advertising strategy is.

STRATEGY

Simply put, advertising strategy is figuring out *what* to say and *how* to say it. AdCracker, a digital advertising training company, explains that a good advertising strategy addresses the problems and opportunities that can have the greatest impact on the brand. This is done in two basic steps: assessment and action. "Assessment" is also the "what" of the advertising strategy. "Action" is the "how." Your assessment comes from deep research about your brand and your potential target audience. Think back to the earlier chapters on the different kinds of research. By now, you should be able to see how important it is to engage in multiple layers of research from different approaches in order to gain as deep an insight as possible into both your brand and your potential consumer.

Take the basic SWOT (strengths, weaknesses, opportunities, and threats) analysis that you learned about in chapter 6. Conducting a SWOT analysis is a systematic way of organizing the findings from your research that helps you better understand the brand, how the brand is viewed by others, and the external situations that can affect your brand and the market. As you organize your research into strengths and weaknesses of the brand, as well as opportunities and threats to the market, you begin to better understand what needs to happen in the advertising that you're recommending to the creative team. Your conviction comes from both your confidence that the research is comprehensive and your understanding of how to apply that research as you connect your target audience to your brand, resulting in the key consumer insight. Note that AdCracker emphasizes the *greatest* impact. In other words, you have to make choices. Your advertising can't connect to *everyone*, and it can't explain *everything* about the brand. One of the paradoxes of advertising is that if you try to do too much, you end up not doing enough. It's yet another reason that ongoing research into your brand and your potential target audience is so critical. You need to have confidence that the *approach* you are choosing for the campaign is the right approach.

It is also important to remember that, especially in the short term, advertising most often solves a *communication* problem. You learned about this in detail in chapter 5. As we discussed earlier, advertising works best when it creates interest, increases awareness, encourages trial, and changes attitudes. That's why it's often recommended that you make sure all aspects of your advertising approach focus on communication. This certainly applies to both the advertising strategy and the advertising objective of your campaign.

While advertising as communication is the stalwart of advertising strategy, some strategists have been arguing recently that working up front to influence behavioral outcomes is a critical way to think of strategy. Adam Ferrier's 2014 book *The Advertising Effect: How to Change Behaviour* is one such example. In it, he argues for behavior motivational strategies on which you can build your advertising strategy. These include (1) utility (advertising as a service), (2) modeling (using aspirational spokespeople), (3) reframing (changing assumptions about the brand), (4) ownership (becoming a part of the advertising campaign), (5) collectivism (reinforcing or creating desirable norms), and (6) play (making the behavior outcome desirable).

As you can see, no exhaustive list of advertising strategies exists, but all provide important guidance for explaining that you must have a clear understanding of what you want the advertising message to achieve. The important thing is that you have a plan—a strategy!

While creating a strategy might seem intuitive, rest assured it is not. Just as with exercise, you don't start out running a marathon. You have to learn how to race 26.2 miles. There are all sorts of plans and exercises to help you achieve your marathon goal. The same is true with advertising strategy. By practicing, you can become better at understanding how to develop an effective advertising strategy. As an advertising student considering a career in account planning, you need to figure out *how* to develop your skills of strategic thinking in order to begin your successful career as an account planner.

One way to develop your strategy skills is to "work backward" with an ad to uncover the original strategy for the advertising. Look at an ad (print ads work well here because you have time to pause and take in the whole ad), and try to figure out the strategy.

Here's a way to begin. Start with figuring out the overt message of the ad. Then take a stab at figuring out the target audience. Then go back and look at the ad again and think about what else you might see. Is your first "reading" of it correct? How do you know? Have you identified the target audience correctly? Continue this cycle until you're convinced you understand the strategy of the advertising. Make sure you can back up your idea of the strategy with sound logic. Well-known advertising professor Dr. Jef I. Richards has said, "Creative without strategy is called 'art.' Creative with strategy is called 'advertising.'" Account planning is the path to smart advertising.

LET'S GIVE THIS A TRY!

A few years ago, the agency Pereira & O'Dell created an advertising campaign for Scrabble that is far from what we might think of as a typical Scrabble ad. Basically, the campaign was a series of ads of "unusual" individuals who needed one more Scrabble piece to get their message across. The ads were developed in a beautiful artistic style that compelled a viewer to stop and contemplate the ad. For example, in one ad, a man is standing in a room that looks like an older train or subway station. He is wearing a sleeveless T-shirt, and his arm is heavily tattooed. His "head" is the *M* square. At the bottom right, there is the Scrabble tray with six of the seven letters there. Which one is missing? The *M*, right? No. Looking at the tray, it only takes a second to realize the *I* is missing. With the *I*, you have the word *mistake*. Hmm. Where is the mistake? Another second of contemplation and you see that his tattoo is of a woman. Oh, her head is the *I*. There. You have it.

Almost. The tag line of the campaign is under the Scrabble tray and reads, "Bringing Letters and People Together."

You start to see that the ad is a little more complicated than you may have originally thought. At first, you may think the campaign is about introducing Scrabble to a new generation of players. Then you realize you already have to understand at least a bit about Scrabble to understand this ad. So maybe the message to the target audience is not about introducing Scrabble. Maybe it's about reintroducing it to former players.

But then you realize it also has to be more than that because it's "Bringing Letters and People Together." Who is supposed to come together in this ad? The woman on the man's tattoo and the man? Oh, but wait. He seems to be in a train station, right? Is he going somewhere? Where is he going? Maybe he's going to find the woman—or find someone else. And maybe they will play Scrabble. Who knows? The people in the ad don't look like typical Scrabble players. Why is that? Perhaps it's to tell the potential consumer that Scrabble is not a "typical" game—and that different kinds of people may play it. And maybe it's not for "everybody," but the question is, is it for you? Now putting all these thoughts together, what do you think is the advertising strategy for this unusual campaign? We can't be sure without talking to the agency people who developed this campaign. But we can make a logical guess.

If we focus on advertising as communication, then we might want to ask ourselves, how is this ad helping to solve a communication problem? We could argue that the advertising strategy for this ad campaign is to *change people's attitudes* about Scrabble and to *remind* them that Scrabble is for everyone—even the unusual people. Or if we use the motivational strategies, we might conclude that this advertising campaign is about *reframing* Scrabble as a game. The combination of tattoos, artistic styling, and unusual location makes reframing a logical conclusion. Even better, however, is to combine the communication strategies with the behavior-outcomes approach and conclude that this advertising campaign is about changing people's attitudes toward playing Scrabble, reminding them that Scrabble is more than a game. In fact, it's reframed as a mechanism for bringing people together.

For another example, let's think about a recent Volkswagen magazine ad. Here is the ad in a nutshell: It's a simple, type-focused ad with a lot of white space. There's no picture of the car. No fancy model. No hairpin, scream-worthy roads. Instead, we see a quote for a headline across the top of the ad: "Brutus, it's good to have you as a friend." The center of the magazine ad is all white space. At the bottom left, the copy reads, "See things before they get dangerous. The Volkswagen Side Assist." Then on the bottom right, you see the logo of VW. That's it. That's the whole ad.

First, let's think about the target audience of this ad. Most likely, the potential consumer is college educated. How do you know this? The headline is a reference to the Shakespeare play *Julius Caesar*. True, you may have actually read the play in high school, but most likely in order to remember this play, you have to have some smarts—and so you go to college. But if the ad is only trying to attract smart people, why choose the *Caesar* quote? After all, if you remember the play, you'll recall that Brutus is about to stab Julius Caesar. Some friend! So now we have to spend some time thinking about why *this* quote is used when the copywriter could have chosen any number of quotes to demonstrate that the Volkswagen is for smart people. The tag line provides the bridge: *See things before they become dangerous.* Caesar is calling Brutus a friend right before he gets stabbed to death. The Volkswagen Side Assist stops things before they get dangerous. And finally, "DON'T DIE. BUY A VOLKSWAGEN."

By now, we're fairly certain that the potential consumer is a smart, college-educated person, but that's hardly a target audience. When you think about this ad, you can begin to see that the ad's approach may be to find the audience who wants a car that is safe (hmm, is this college-aged person married with a family?) but has the time to remember things like Shakespeare plays. Probably the potential consumer has a white-collar job that requires contemplation but is at least a little bit interesting. And this audience probably needs to know enough about VW that they don't require a whole lot of information other than to be introduced to this new *safety* feature. And remember, with only a few clever phrases, safety is really the hero of this ad.

It's important to also understand that the strategy of the ad may include other aspects besides brand position and target audience. The creators of this ad have most likely thought long and hard about figuring out a way to get the consumer to stop at this ad and contemplate the meaning—if only for a moment. This is one reason that what we think of as "legacy" advertising continues to be important to the whole POEM (paid, owned, and earned media) mix of advertising. While images come flying at us from every corner of the media world, it becomes more and more difficult for any of those images to stick.

Think back to chapter 2 and the discussion about advertising clutter. The forward-thinking advertising strategists know this is a challenge, but they have the tools and understanding to thrive in this cluttered environment. Chapter 1 describes a potential checklist to consider when thinking about whether you would make a good account planner. A basic knowledge of neuroscience is especially helpful in understanding advertising strategy. "Filling in the gaps" is a concept in the literature that helps us understand how the brain works. In the persuasion literature, for example, there's a form of speech called the syllogism—a rhetorical device for making an argument. There are lots of different kinds of syllogisms, but for this ad, the syllogism that emphasizes the premise that the audience supplies the missing information is particularly helpful. There are all sorts of things that are left out of this ad, things that the consumer has to supply in order for the ad to make sense. The psychology behind this is that the advertisement is more persuasive *because* of this missing information. The brain has to work hard to make the connection, and when it does, it's powerful.

If you think back to chapter 5 and the discussion about brand positioning, in this ad, perhaps you can see that the positioning statement might be "For the thoughtful and contemplative parent, Volkswagen is the only one that delivers safety that you can stake a friendship on, because only Volkswagen cars are equipped with Side Assist technology." It's a little bit awkward, but you can begin to see where the strategy for the ad might be. If this is the *positioning* that Volkswagen is striving for, what is the *strategy* that will get them there?

If you think back to the earlier discussion of thinking of strategy simply as *what* to say and *how* to say it, then you could argue that the strategy of this ad is to help the target audience to aspire to be smart enough to buy a VW (the what to say) and to do it in a simple but clever, pause-for-a-moment manner (how to say it).

Advertising, when done with care, precision, and multiple layers of meaning, as in the examples of the Scrabble and Volkswagen ads, can leave a lasting impact on the potential consumer. And isn't that ultimately what we are always trying to do?

SUGGESTED ACTIVITIES
TO HELP YOU THINK ABOUT THIS CHAPTER

Activity 1: Pick an ad from a magazine that you don't usually read. Now work backward from the execution to the strategy behind the ad. Ask yourself:
- What is the overt message of the ad?
- Who is the target audience?
- Do they match up?
- Does this ad fit the audience that reads this magazine? If yes, then explain how. If no, then explain why not.

Activity 2: Pick a brand that your parents might use but you don't. Look at ads for this brand and for its competition. Are they speaking to the same target audience? Or are these brands really reaching out to different people? Write a target profile for the three different brands for a similar product. Where are they similar? And where do they diverge?

Activity 3: Walk around your room (or apartment or house), and pick a product that you use every day. What is the benefit of this product? That is, what does it do for you, the consumer? How can you sell that benefit in a headline and one image?

REFERENCES

Ferrier, A. (2014). *The advertising effect: How to change behaviour.* South Melbourne, Australia: Oxford University Press.

CHAPTER 11

Your Brand's Best Advertising Approach

As mentioned in chapter 10, strategy is simply figuring out what you need to say and how you're planning to say it. It's important to remember that you don't create the strategy out of nothing, or as some might say, out of thin air. Rather, you need to take the knowledge about advertising that you've accumulated and the information that you've gathered from your research and apply it toward an understanding of how to approach the advertising that you're recommending to the creative group.

While advertising has fundamentally changed over the decades, it's still important to learn from the past before moving into the future. A few advertising models help in this regard.

One popular model that relates to advertising strategy is the Foote, Cone & Belding (FCB) grid. Developed by FCB executive Richard Vaughn in 1980, the FCB grid can help you understand that different product categories tend to resonate in people's minds differently. For example, buying salt doesn't take much thought. You don't buy it that often, it doesn't cost much, and the consequences aren't that catastrophic if you buy the wrong salt. Cars, however, are a different story. They cost a lot more than salt, and if you make a wrong decision, you may be stuck with a lemon for many years. While researchers have tweaked the model throughout the years, here's a basic outline for the FCB grid.

	Think	Feel
High involvement	Quadrant 1	Quadrant 2
Low involvement	Quadrant 3	Quadrant 4

Notice there are four quadrants. The model looks at two basic dimensions: emotion (think versus feel) and involvement (high versus low). The four quadrants are: think/high involvement; think/low involvement; feel/high involvement; and feel/low involvement. There are all sorts of versions of this grid—and all offer something helpful. Historically, the FCB grid focused on product categories. It's certainly logical to do so. You would expect to see insurance companies in one category (think/high involvement) and a candy bar in a different one (feel/low involvement).

However, you should now have an understanding that advertising is often more about positioning one brand against another rather than just positioning category against category. You should also have enough of an understanding now to figure out that "insurance" might be emotional for certain consumers. What if you're buying insurance for your first house, for example? And while a candy bar ought not to generate much involvement, what if you've been on a diet for months and finally decide to blow it and grab your favorite treat? That could be a high-involvement decision. So how can the FCB grid help us develop an appropriate advertising strategy?

While it's often true that product categories fit into one category over another, it can be helpful to think about the brand you're representing differently. For example, where is the most typical quadrant you would expect to find your brand category? Now, based on some preliminary research, does it make sense to move your brand closer to a different quadrant? Or possibly to a different quadrant altogether? If so, why? Using the FCB grid to help you see your brand in a new light can help you better understand how the advertising strategy you're helping to develop can break through the "expected" advertising and tell a different—and more compelling—story. Let's use the category "insurance" again and follow some strategic thinking. In your secondary and primary research, you discover two important insights: (1) People are more worried about insurance than you had previously thought, and (2) insurance choices are more often wrapped up in emotional decisions—decisions that can be hindered because of the stress of the cost of the product. This information tells you that your insurance brand most likely resides in a "high involvement" category. If you're worried, you need to get more information to deal with the worry. However, you've also discovered that while you expect potential consumers to deal with the worry then make a rational decision (the classic "high involvement/ high thinking" quadrant), more research indicates that isn't usually what happens. You examine the most popular advertisements about insurance —some of these are direct competitors of your brand. You realize that many of the advertisements have a strategy that dismisses your potential target audience's worry. You believe your brand should be a "thinking" product as well as a "high involvement" product, but your research indicates that consumers have a hard time thinking about your brand because their emotions get in the way. How do you deal with that? Flo from Progressive basically tells you that you don't have to worry because Progressive will put all the information together. Allstate Insurance also tells you not to worry because "You're in Good Hands." But you decide (and you believe you have the research to back it up) that rather than just worry, your consumers need more information in order to choose the right insurance. They don't want to just be in good hands. They want the tools to better understand their insurance options.

Other advertising models can also provide launching pads to help you think more clearly—and more strategically—about your brand. Here are a few that can be particularly helpful.

HIERARCHY OF EFFECTS MODEL

This model is often called simply the "think/feel/do" model. Researchers break this down in numerous ways, but primarily the idea is that you have to first introduce *awareness* of the brand, then help your target audience gain more *knowledge* about the brand, help them develop their *preference* for your brand, get them to the point that they have a *conviction* about your brand, and eventually hope they will *purchase* the brand. Most likely you'll need to zero in on one aspect of this model—and your research should help you figure out strategically which makes the most sense. For example, if you're the account planner for Fage yogurt, your research has shown you that your consumers know a lot about yogurt but not a lot about Greek yogurt, and they have little knowledge that Fage is one of the few brands that actually has a Greek heritage. You decide that you can create knowledge, preference, and conviction with one advertising campaign because, in part, you've discovered that your target audience, when presented with important ingredient information, can not only build preference for Fage but also develop the conviction that this is the only brand their family members will eat. So you build your strategy on the concept that the right information about Greek yogurt yields appropriate conviction on the authenticity of Fage.

While hierarchy of effects models can help you think strategically about your brand, these models aren't perfect. The basis of the model is one of logical progression. On the surface, that makes perfect sense, right? After all, as humans we are rational. Or so we would like to think. How many times have you bought something first and then developed emotions about it? Probably more times than you would like to admit. Perhaps you've heard the old adage, "Do we eat whole wheat bread because we like it? Or do we like it because we eat it?" Advertising is built on connecting the brand to the consumer, and that connection often occurs because of emotion that, more times than not, is less than completely rational. So, use the hierarchy of effects model as a way to understand that there are lots of components to an effective ad—and your campaign may need to focus on one facet more than the other.

SOCIAL LEARNING THEORY

From an advertising perspective, social learning theory tells us that we learn from what we see in the media. This includes the advertisements we are exposed to. This theory gained popularity back in the 1960s with the "Bobo Doll" experiment (Bandura, 1977). Here is a brief description of this experiment: Young children watched adults hit a Bobo Doll (a large, freaky, clown-like blow-up toy). Then they had the opportunity to "play" with the doll. Those who had watched the adults would hit the Bobo Doll at a higher rate than those who were in the control group (children who had not witnessed adults hitting the doll). Hundreds of studies followed (many criticizing the Bobo Doll experiment), including studies that showed how social learning theory applies to what we see in advertisements.

From the account planner's perspective, it's important, first, to understand the impact that advertising can have on your target audience. Social learning theory shows us how strong a message can be. So at the very least, it's important to understand that every item in the ad—choice of actors, position of the brand, type fonts, and background colors—everything will have some kind of influence on the potential consumer. It's yet another reason deep, insightful research is so important to the advertising campaign.

Second, it's also important to understand that the consumer's reaction to the ad may be subtle, small, and unnoticeable to the average person (including the consumers themselves). But that doesn't mean the ad is ineffective. Advances in neuroscience have helped us understand that we're even more complicated than we have previously thought. For those working in advertising, this is important. For example, scientists know a lot more about *implicit memory* than they used to. Without getting too technological, you can think of implicit memory as ideas and pictures sitting in our brains unbeknown to us. Without thinking about it, we do all sorts of things "automatically." Think about going out for a walk, for example. While you might have to decide where to go, what shoes to wear, and how long you want to be outside, what you typically don't have to do is think about the walking itself. You typically don't say, "Hmm, do I start with my left foot or my right foot? After one foot moves, what do I do with the other foot?" That's your implicit memory working. At one time, you *did* have to think about it. But now, it's automatic. If you know someone who has suffered a traumatic brain injury, you may have had to watch that person "relearn" all sorts of things, such as walking and eating. But if your brain is working properly, you're doing all sorts of things you aren't thinking about. That's because these tasks are embedded deep inside our brains as part of our implicit memory.

From an advertising perspective, this is important. For example, understanding implicit memory helps account planners better understand that the advertising campaign they are working on is part of the brand's "history." Everything that happened before (good and bad) matters. Everything that happens in the future will be affected—even if it's just a little bit—by the current campaign. Think about a typical trip to the grocery store to buy peanut butter, soap, and cereal. The choices, the choices! If you didn't have the benefit of implicit memory, it would be incredibly stressful to walk the aisles trying to choose brands. Even if you don't choose Jif, your brain may help you remember that "Choosy Mothers Choose Jif." You can store that away and draw on it when making your new choice.

Implicit memory is also important to the account planner because it helps us understand that we can't make wholesale changes to our brands without acknowledging the past advertising. Even if a brand is ready to be taken in an entirely new direction, the consuming public will have feelings about the brand that have to be considered. It's just one reason you often see campaigns moving forward in smaller increments as they build toward consumer loyalty. Cola products are excellent examples of this. Through the years, Pepsi and Coca-Cola have run many campaigns, rolling out new tag lines, introducing new brands. But if you look at these brands closely, you begin to see that the strong loyalty consumers have toward one brand over the other isn't because of any one campaign but rather due to an ongoing history of campaigns.

Third, understanding the basic concept behind implicit memory also helps us understand that seemingly unimportant parts of an ad may have "memory triggers" to a potential consumer. Associating the color green with "go" and red with "stop" is due to implicit memory. So if you use red as a primary color in a campaign, you have to understand that a consumer may think "stop." This could be good (as in "stop and think about this for a moment") or bad (as in "stop, don't buy this brand"). It doesn't mean that red is off limits (who would want to tell Coca-Cola that?). But you should to be aware of the ramifications of color choice.

If account planners are keeping up on the latest research (and they should), they're better able to help the creatives understand the choices that they make in developing the most effective advertising campaign possible.

COGNITIVE DISSONANCE THEORY

From an account planner's perspective, cognitive dissonance theory can shed light on the impact of advertising in a way that isn't always considered.

The theory is usually attributed to Leon Festinger. Here's the idea behind cognitive dissonance theory: If I spend a lot of time thinking about something, I need justification that it was time well spent. Or if I spend a lot of money on something, I need to believe that I spent my money wisely. If I'm unsure, I have "dissonance." (Have you ever thought, "Wow, that was a total waste of money" after buying something?) The theory argues that people don't like dissonance and need to do something to get rid of it. There are at least two important ways to get rid of dissonance that has ramifications for advertisers and their brands. The first is for the consumers to contemplate just how great a decision they made. Here is their thinking: "Sure, it was a lot of money—and for a moment, I may have thought it was a waste of money. But as I'm remembering my love for this product, I'm now remembering that it doesn't matter how much it cost. I love it!"

The second way cognitive dissonance theory can work is that the consumers simply change their mind about the product. So instead of thinking, "That was a waste of money," cognitive theory argues that if you change your mind ("Wow, that was a bargain"), you'll get rid of the dissonance. It's one reason advertising theorists explain why people, after purchasing an expensive product like an automobile, will start looking at advertisements featuring their car—but also the competition's products—to help justify that the money spent was a good idea. If account planners are aware of cognitive dissonance theory, when digging into the potential target audience's psyche, they can make a judgment call on whether creating an ad that focuses on cognitive dissonance would resonate with the consumer. On the surface, you might think this ought to be avoided. But the theory argues that if there is dissonance and the dissonance is resolved, the person involved will be more persuaded by whatever caused the dissonance in the first place. Now, can you imagine some scenarios where creating that kind of dissonance might be a brilliant and innovative approach for the advertising that you recommend to the creative team?

FOOT-IN-THE-DOOR THEORY

Also in the 1960s, researchers (Freedman & Fraser, 1966) developed an experiment that showed if you asked someone to do something small and inconsequential, you could come back later and ask for something much more complicated. The experiment was rather novel. Researchers in California asked people to put big, ugly signs in their front yards to promote the idea of keeping their neighborhood beautiful. It was no surprise that people refused. Then they asked people to put a small placard in their front window giving the same message. Neighbors agreed. But then, two weeks later, they returned to the neighbors who agreed to put the small placards on their windows and asked them to put the same big, ugly signs in their front yard, and many people agreed.

From an advertising perspective, it's easy to see how this could be important for your advertising strategy. Are you trying to get the consumer to make a major brand change? If so, your advertising strategy might be to start out asking the consumer to make a small change. Perhaps it's simply to try the new brand. Or to add something to a regular purchase. Or to think about different flavors of a favorite brand. If you're using the foot-in-the-door theory to inform your advertising strategy, you're most likely thinking in several steps, which could be a brilliant way to unveil a new brand or brand design.

Ultimately, all these advertising theories are helpful only if they help you, the account planner, gain insights into the consumer's thinking process as it relates to the brand. Remember that a theory is simply a lens that helps you see more clearly. But seeing more clearly can lead to stronger—and more creative—advertising.

SUGGESTED ACTIVITIES
TO HELP YOU THINK ABOUT THIS CHAPTER

Activity 1: Create an FCB grid on an 11 × 8½ piece of paper (that is, make the page horizontal). Now walk around your dorm room, apartment, or house choosing different things you see. Where would they fit on the FCB grid? Write on the grid where you would place each item.

Activity 2: Now create another FCB grid on an 11 × 8½ piece of paper. This time choose one product and consider all the different brands for that product. Where would you place each of those brands on the FCB grid?

Activity 3: Think about the cognitive dissonance model. Now think about a time when you bought something that, at the time, you didn't think it was a great deal but you later justified as a good deal. How did you think about that decision then? And how do you think about that decision now?

REFERENCES

Bandura, A. (1977). Self-efficacy: Toward a unifying theory of behavioral change. *Psychological Review, 84,* 191–215.

Festinger, L. (1957). *A theory of cognitive dissonance.* Stanford, CA: Stanford University Press.

Freedman, J. L., & Fraser, S. C. (1966). Compliance without pressure: The foot in the door technique. *Journal of Personality and Social Psychology, 4,* 195–202.

Vaugh, R. (1980). How advertising works: A planning model. *Journal of Advertising Research, 20,* 27–30.

CHAPTER 12

Concept Testing

How to Figure Out If You're Heading Down the Right Advertising Path

This chapter builds on the research methods that you learned in earlier chapters. It shows you how to use these methods to "concept test" a proposed advertising approach.

You may feel confident in your advertising approach, but it's always a good idea to "double-check." Your brand's client will be spending a lot of money on this advertising, and you want to do everything you can to make sure the campaign will succeed. Even before the creative work is developed and you hand off the project to the creative team, it's critical to be as confident as possible in your recommendations.

As an account planner, you will most likely be involved in research throughout your brand's advertising campaign. In previous chapters, you learned about different research methods that are helpful as you work to uncover insights for your brand and your potential consumers. But the research doesn't stop there. You will most likely also be asked to perform some research shortly before the campaign launches. This is known as "concept testing." And even after that the research may not be over. If the budget allows, you might conduct research during the campaign. There are several reasons for this. First, you may discover that the campaign is even more successful than anticipated. In that case, you (and perhaps your counterpart from the media department) may recommend an expanded campaign. Or perhaps the campaign isn't going as planned and, rather than wait it out, you want to see if you can make corrections or end the campaign early.

You may even be called on to conduct research after the advertising campaign has run its course. At the very least, you and your colleagues will conduct some kind of "postmortem," which is simply reviewing the campaign and discussing what went well with the campaign and what could be improved. If the budget allows, you might interview some consumers who were in the target audience as you investigate whether the advertising approach reached its potential audience in the way you had hoped.

This chapter, however, focuses on concept testing before the campaign runs: the kind of quirky research that helps you tweak, confirm, or strengthen your advertising recommendations to the creative team.

So first, let's review what you want the creative team to believe about the advertising approach you're recommending.

Target audience. You need to know, without a doubt, that the advertising you're recommending will reach your target audience. As discussed previously, most likely when you started your research, you already knew the basic demographics of whom this advertising should reach. For example, the client may have told you that the campaign needs to convince men who have retired before their full Social Security age that T. Rowe Price has wealth managers standing ready to help them navigate the common pitfalls of early retirement years. That is your target *market*. But who among this group is your target *audience*? Your extensive research has uncovered that there is a subgroup of these men who are spirited individuals. These are adventurous, yet somewhat cautious, men who, though open to talking with a wealth manager, are hesitant because of their reluctance to join a group. How might concept testing help you shore up your understanding of this target audience?

Advertising objective. You have learned that an advertising objective can only solve an advertising problem. Therefore, your recommendations for the advertising campaign should focus on communication. Based on the example above, your research indicates that this campaign should focus on *building awareness* of what T. Rowe Price wealth managers can offer the individual retirement investor. You've found out what the target audience knows about wealth management. You've made a decision about the key points of wealth management that your campaign should stress. You've uncovered four key elements, but your research indicates that your target audience is only going to listen to one of them. Are you sure you've pinpointed the most relevant element?

Advertising strategy. As your research has developed, you've zeroed in on the right target audience, and you've decided what information you'll emphasize for your awareness campaign. But you have to decide *how* you'll present these ideas to your target audience. Should the campaign be humorous, serious, or emotional? Should it be simple or more sophisticated? Your research shows that this target audience likes to laugh—even though retirement investing is far from funny. So just how funny do you want your campaign to be? How can concept testing help you determine the limits of humor that you want to consider?

Because of all the research you've conducted, you should feel confident about these key areas. However, even if you're convinced you've approached the recommended campaign appropriately (and by this time, you really should be convinced), it's important to remember that there is always some aspect to tweak and make better, some nuance that you want to develop, or some new way to define the target audience. This is where concept testing comes in.

APPROACHING CONCEPT TESTING

You've already learned about an array of research methodologies to draw on when learning more about your brand or your consumer. However, even though the research methodologies may be the same, your approach is different when conducting a concept test.

For example, suppose you've developed a consumer persona to represent your target audience. Think back to the *consumer persona* concept described in chapter 5. Let's say you're working with a persona and you've described him as someone who enjoys hiking the Appalachian Trail alone. Hmm. Are you sure the Appalachian Trail is correct? Maybe the South Rim of the Grand Canyon will resonate better. Both destinations represent the same kind of person. Sort of. But one location might resonate with your target audience more than another. What to do?

This is where concept testing can help. You have all sorts of ways to go about this. Here are a few examples. Find a group of people who are in your target audience; get them together and do a *brainstorming exercise*. There are lots of ways this can work. Here are two examples.

Mind Mapping

One popular brainstorming exercise is to "mind map" a word, phrase, or concept to see if any new patterns emerge. You could do this in a group with those in the target audience, with members of your own account team, or with other groups of people who might offer important insights that could relate to your brand.

Simply put, mind mapping is a visual way to connect ideas to each other. There are plenty of free templates available online to help you get started, but you don't really need a template. All you need is either a big sheet of paper or a whiteboard to help you "go with the flow."

Start with your word, phrase, or idea that you're trying to develop, and write it in the middle of the space. With the example above, you might write "favorite nature spots" or "best vacation ever" or even "must visit before I die." Then ask for input, but ask without judging. Write down everything that your participants offer. Once you have some phrases, start seeing if you can make some connections and then build off of those. It's a process of "free-flowing ideas" while also analyzing results. In order for this to work, you need at least one other person to brainstorm with. As you work together to uncover the best destination for your advertising campaign, with mind mapping the key is to reserve judgment, share ideas, write things down, analyze, talk, analyze some more—and see where it takes you. You might just be surprised at some of the ideas that come out.

Positioning as Brainstorming

Do you remember how we examined the FCB grid in chapter 11? You can take that same basic idea and draw a grid with opposite explanations on both the X-axis and the Y-axis.

For example, if you want to better understand the parameters of travel destinations for your target audience, on the X-axis you might write "Caribbean cruise" on the left side and "White-water rafting" on the right side. On the Y-axis, you might write "Spare no expense" on the top side and "Can I get it for free?" on the bottom side. For the brainstorming exercise, you could ask people in your target audience to position themselves on the grid. Or you could ask them to position something else that might relate to your brand (e.g., "retirement plans") on the axis. Or you could ask them to place all the competitors that you uncovered in your secondary and primary research on the grid. The point is to get a number of different ideas and then look and contemplate insights that relate to your advertising strategy.

You can also use more traditional research methods for your concept testing. For example, if you're trying to decide between the Appalachian Trail and the Grand Canyon South Rim as possible symbolic destinations for the creative team to consider, you can uncover opinions using research methods that you learned in chapters 8 and 9.

You might choose a simple question such as, "If you had a week, would you rather hike the Appalachian Trail or the South Rim?" You could ask this to lots of people via social media, or you could have small groups explore the benefits of each destination in a focus group. The point is, with concept testing you have a specific issue for which you're trying to garner more insights. Concept testing isn't the time to ask your target audience about how many times a week they purchase your brand, or how often they like to be outdoors. You already know that. Concept testing is about confirming your approach or making important adjustments before thousands of dollars are spent on the advertising campaign.

Depending on time and budget constraints, you may not have time to test every nuance of your advertising approach. If time or budget is limited, review your research and then make the call. Do you need to know more about the target audience, the advertising objective, or the advertising strategy? Is there some aspect of the campaign that you just have to know is the absolute best approach? For example, once you've settled on a bit of cautious "adventure" for your enthusiastic, yet hesitant, retirement investor, you know you want to push (a bit) on intellectual athleticism. Your research tells you sailing might be appropriate, but you don't want to move into advertising clichés with pictures of the America's Cup racers chopping through the waves. But perhaps "navigate" is the right word to build your concept. You want to show a boat, perhaps, but which one? An old wooden dory? A canoe? A rowing scull? Here is how you could test this using different research techniques you've already learned.

Focus Groups

We talked about focus groups in chapter 9. Here's a way to apply concept testing. Gather a group that fits your target audience as closely as possible. To continue with the reticent adventurous retirement investor, you're looking for people who are as close to this as you can find—not just men in their 60s who have retired but also men who fit your target audience. How will you find them? Chances are, you personally don't know a lot of them. But maybe your parents do (or maybe your father fits). Find one. Ask him to find another. And so on. This is called "snowball sample" or "snowballing." While not randomly generated, pinpointing people who fit your target audience can give you a wealth of important insights. You don't need a lot of people to help you zero in on the right concept. Six to ten people can be ideal. Once you have your focus group, the process is similar to what you already learned in chapter 9. Just make sure the questions you ask deal with what you're trying to test. Remember: An old wooden dory? A canoe? A scull? This is not the time to ask about how much they would spend on a retirement adviser.

Once your group is assembled, after introductions you could start by asking them, "When you think of boats, what kind of boats come to mind?" Try to keep the conversation open, and get them to list all the boats they can think of. Don't judge—and don't push. For example, don't say, "What about a canoe? Do you ever think about a canoe?"

After you get the list of all the boats, take a quick look at which boats were mentioned and if participants nodded or said "me too" when someone mentioned that particular boat. From there, you could ask them to help you understand why they thought of these boats. Listen carefully. Take notes. (You should also be recording the conversation.)

After all that, you can show them a list of the boats you're considering. (Of course, if no one mentioned these boats in the previous discussion, you may need to go over some explanation of why you still want to ask them about these particular boats.) Ask them which is their favorite. Ask them to rank order them. Ask them to think of a word for each of the boats. And this is just the beginning. For concept testing, you have to put your best creative hat on and ask questions in unusual ways in order to uncover some little snippet of information that may help your already-great campaign move up a notch from great to fabulous.

Word Associations

We also touched on word associations in chapter 9, but there are all sorts of ways you can use word associations for concept testing as well. For example, you could take words (*navigate*) on which you're considering anchoring your concept and try them out on the target audience. There are endless ways to do this. You could use the word *navigate* and choose an opposite word (perhaps *aimless*) and ask people in your target audience to position your brand somewhere between the two words (as in the grid above). Or you could ask participants to list all the words they think of when they hear the word *navigate* and see what kind of patterns emerge that might relate to your target audience, your objective, your strategy, or even the brand itself.

Surveys

After learning about options such as Likert statements, random selection, and double-barreled questions in chapter 8, it may be a little disconcerting to approach surveys completely differently by the time you get to the concept-testing stage. But surveys you conduct to discover important information while you're zeroing in on the target audience or trying to connect consumers to the brand take a different approach than when you have strong convictions and are merely trying to eke out any remaining insights—or you need to confirm what you've discovered. So let's go back to our example of "which boat is better." If you were conducting a survey for the concept test, the question might look like this:

Imagine you have one day to spend on the water and do anything you would like. On which boat would you choose to spend your day on the water?

A. An old wooden, handcrafted New England dory
B. A "camp green" canoe
C. A racing scull

Perhaps you would even include a photo of each to help participants understand the differences of each kind of boat.

With surveys, you can take the opportunity to explore creative approaches or to gather data from lots of people who might help you with your concept refinement. For example, for the question above, you might decide to see if slight differences in your target audience affect which answer is chosen. You may have zeroed in on men who have been retired for two years or fewer. A two-year spread, even for an explicit target audience, might yield slightly different results. So you ask the respondent his age. (You already know that you're targeting men between the ages of 63 and 66.) You discover, to your surprise, that 66-year-olds tended to pick the racing shell more often than 63-year-olds. You can't conclude this if you've asked five people this question (as opposed to five people in a focus group who may be enough to yield interesting results). However, the more data you gather, the easier it is to see the pattern.

The point is that at this stage in the strategy development, you should be so attuned to your brand and your brand's potential consumer that trying some of these creative research approaches in the concept-testing phase can help you further fine-tune your approach. You're trying to get at some specific piece of information.

Ultimately, regardless of the concept you're testing at this point in the advertising strategy development, you're most likely concentrating on one or more of these areas:

Persuasiveness. Persuading people about your concept isn't necessarily about persuading them to buy the product. It would typically be more along the lines of persuading the consumer to change brands, to try the product, or to buy more of the product. In order to know whether your concept is persuasive, you need to evaluate before you introduce them to the concept so you know it is this concept rather than something else that has persuaded them.

Likeability. Likeability typically looks at how well the consumer likes the advertising concept as a whole or a particular part of the concept. To discover this information, you can simply ask an open-ended question such as, "When you read the description of the advertising concept, how do you think you'll like the ad when you see it? Why?"

Attention. If the advertising your creative team does isn't attention getting, it runs the risk of fading into the background before anyone is persuaded by it. You have to figure out if the idea you're pursuing will garner the kind of attention your brand deserves. You can simply ask your respondents, "How well does this concept hold your attention?" Or you could ask them to explain to you what the concept means as a way to better understand whether they've paid the appropriate attention to the ad.

The dilemma is that you could do all kinds of research forever and never be really certain you know the best strategy for your advertising campaign. But you have to trust that you've done the best research possible with the resources available. And then go out on a limb, make a decision, and sell it to the creative team. The creative team is eagerly waiting to hear what insights you've uncovered.

SUGGESTED ACTIVITIES
TO HELP YOU THINK ABOUT THIS CHAPTER

Activity 1: Create a mind map for a product that you use regularly. It might be a brand of toothpaste, a place you like to eat, or any number of other things. Draw the mind map on a large piece of paper or a whiteboard. Be sure you look for new connections between different points. Take a photo of your finished mind map so you can document your thinking and share with others working on your team.

Activity 2: Positioning can also become a brainstorming technique. Think of two opposites for two different points of interest for your target audience. Your X-axis might be a *place* and your Y-axis might be *cost*. Or if you're exploring travel, one might be *meaningful* and the other how *fun*. Of course you can come up with creative names for the opposite end points. Now start asking those in your target audience to plot different points on your grid based on the two axes. And ask why they plotted these as they did. What does this tell you?

Activity 3: Word associations can both be fun and lead to new ideas. Take five words that you might use as you develop your campaign; then start making lists of all the words you might think of related to each of those five words. Note that this is also a technique that some copywriters use to ensure they have the right word. Of course a good thesaurus is also a handy tool.

CHAPTER 13

Finally, Heading to the Creative Brief

By the time you read this chapter, you should have the tools and the data to make sound decisions on the direction of the advertising for which you're responsible. You're now ready for one of the most important tasks for which the account planner is responsible: spearheading the creative brief. The culmination of the account planner is developing the creative brief. This chapter will explain what a creative brief is, why it's important, and how to develop one.

WHAT IS THE CREATIVE BRIEF?

By now, you should have a good idea about the importance of the creative brief. Everything you've learned from this book so far ultimately feeds into the creative brief. So it is understandable if you've figured out the basics of what constitutes the creative brief. But even if you have, we haven't yet dealt with the specifics of what does and doesn't go into the brief.

Simply put, the creative brief is a short document that tells the creative team how to proceed with the creative development of the advertising campaign. It is common for the account planner to take responsibility of developing the creative brief. Think of the brief as a map for the creative team. They aren't required to follow it, but it provides important information; indeed, if the team ignores this information, they could drift off course. While each advertising agency has its own version of the creative brief, at the very least they all touch on these elements: (1) the target audience, (2) the brand's position, (3) what the advertising needs to accomplish, and (4) where the agency's message will run.

The research you've conducted up to this point is what gives you the confidence to construct the creative brief. It's important to remember, however, that the research never stops. You must continue to analyze the data from your research and be open minded enough to learn new insights while developing the creative brief. The challenge for the account planner is to summarize the research in such a way that it incorporates the key insights and provides enough convincing evidence—without spending too much time explaining how you arrived at your conclusions. After all, there's a reason this is called a *brief*.

Agencies all have their own approach to synthesizing research and insights to inform the advertising strategy and the creative brief. For example, Grey Advertising (part of the WPP group) recently added the question "How can we make the idea reflect and respect the world's diversity?" to every creative brief. In an *Ad Age* article, Grey Worldwide creative officer John Patroulis explained that the agency was adding a question to the brief to "ensure that agency staffers—as well as clients collaborating on creative—discuss diversity and fairness at the beginning of an idea, which will help the work better reflect the world and its consumers" (Stein, 2018). Adding a diversity question to the creative brief isn't a haphazard decision. Rather, it demonstrates that advertising developed by Grey Advertising is communication that considers multiple points of view. Given that advertising is typically geared toward dealing in segments of like-minded people (the target audience), this is an important statement that can help the creative team understand a specific advertising challenge within a global environment.

The Internet provides all sorts of examples of creative briefs. One site to consider is workamajig.com. On this site, Sheila Moses offers a blog post that describes the fundamentals of a creative brief. She also posts examples of briefs from Hush Puppies, Reebok, Quaker Oats, and PayPal. While each of these briefs has a lot in common, there are also key differences among them. For example, the Reebok brief is type heavy and straightforward, focusing on what needs to be done and how to achieve the objective. While the Quaker Oats brief also focuses on the fundamentals, it does so in a more creative and art-heavy way. The layout, graphics, and fonts of the brief all help tell the story of what the advertising is trying to accomplish. The point here is that there is no one way to create a brief as long as you remember that the brief is the map that will help your creatives navigate the best advertising for the client.

One brief that we have found particularly helpful for a variety of brands is Faris Yakob's "Idea Brief." We like this brief because of its forward thinking and understanding of the social media landscape. You can find Yakob's illuminating brief at https://farisyakob.typepad.com/files/a-new-brief-faris -yakob.pdf. While this brief shares similarities with most other creative briefs, we like it because it focuses on insights, which are key to uniting the brand and the consumer. Yakob's brief highlights four "insights": (1) the community insight, (2) the brand insight, (3) the culture insights, and (4) the social insight.

Community Insight

Yakob describes the community insight as finding out what matters most to the community with which your brand wishes to engage. This "community" can encompass many ideas. For example, the community might be part of the target audience's "tribe" on social media. Or it could include actual communities in which many of the target audience members live. It could be a place of worship, or an educational system. It could be a community of people who have banded together around an environmental issue. As an account planner, you should be so knowledgeable about the community (or communities) in which your target audience lives that you can succinctly state the most important insight about a key community that will help the creatives develop the advertising campaign.

Brand Insight

The brand insight is the brand's point of view. The idea brief asks you to think about how the brand behaves in the world in the way that only this particular brand can. To uncover the most important brand insight, by now you should be able to think of the brand as a personality. You should know how the brand views the world. For example, how would your brand feel if it could no longer provide financial help to those in need in the communities in which the brand is most appreciated? As odd as it might sound to think of your brand as a personality, if you have the research to back up your position (and you should if you've done your homework), you should be able to confidently explain the brand insight. With the brand insight, you're trying to clearly (and creatively) state the brand's position in relation to all other brands that might be viewed as competition.

Culture Insight

The culture insight asks you to think about what is currently happening in the culture that you can capitalize on to connect to the brand. This is where white papers and trend reports can be particularly helpful. Being mindful of what is happening in the culture that might help illuminate your brand requires both research skills and an ability to think creatively about seemingly unconnected ideas. It might be a subtle connection, but it can be profound.

For example, when Hurricane Florence hit the Carolinas in September 2018, State Farm Insurance ran an ad that named past hurricanes (Ike, Andres, Rita, and Sandy) and then, in the same voice-over, named State Farm employees Chris, Jackie, Joe, and Shannon. The commercial ended with the tag line "We're a force of nature too." While at first glance it might not seem that this commercial has tapped into "culture," it's possible that the culture of uncertainty and anxiety that many have argued has plagued us in recent years is addressed in this advertising approach. The culture-insight section of the idea brief could have read something like, "No matter how difficult things get in the 'culture divide' we're experiencing, State Farm is there to offer a comforting hand. Real people tackling real problems."

Social Insight

The social insight section asks you to think about how the brand is discussed in social media. This is where your social media monitoring becomes particularly important. You should be able to make some connections by monitoring the social space so you know who the brand's influencers are and how the brand is welcomed into the social media community.

While many of these "insights" may be incorporated into other agency creative briefs, the focus of insights in Yakob's "Idea Brief" helps the account planner remember that the fundamental goal of the advertising approach is to uncover the key consumer insight and connect it to the key brand insight in order to create effective advertising.

AFTER THE CREATIVE BRIEF IS COMPLETED

Congratulations. You've developed a well-crafted creative brief. Now it's time to convince those who will actually develop the advertising campaign that you've discovered the right approach. If all has gone well, you will have had conversations with the creative group all along the process so they're aware of the direction you're hoping to move the advertising. You want the creative team to be as eager to flesh out the campaign as you are to hand them the reins and see your research efforts bear fruit. But your job is not done yet. Even if you aren't required to make an official pitch to the creative team, your creative brief needs to be written in such a way that it serves as a pitch on its own.

Creative briefs are typically short. It isn't unusual for the brief to be one page. Even though you have reams of data to support your ideas, you'll need to boil the data down into pithy phrases that give the sense of what the advertising ought to do. How you write the brief is as important as the ideas you're putting forth. For example, the title section of Yakob's "Idea Brief" is called "In Brief." It's a one-line summary that captures the essence of the brief.

If you were in charge of the Pellegrino brand, for example, you would need to begin your brief with some kind of summary. "Creative Brief for Advertising Approach for Pellegrino Water," while perhaps factual, doesn't capture the heart of the brief. "Pellegrino Conquers the Fashion World" may be better. It depends, of course, on what your research has uncovered. It's better to think of this one-line summary as a tag line than as a title.

When the time comes to present the creative brief, there are myriad ways this may happen. If the creatives haven't been involved in the process of developing the brief, you may be asked to give a formal pitch to the creative department and others who may decide to watch the presentation. Or the "pitch" could be informal, a sitting-around-the-table kind of experience where you're asked questions and share your thoughts and concerns as everyone pours over the brief that you've written. Whatever the process is at your particular agency, three ideas tend to be consistent. First, you should be confident. Remember, you've done the research. At this point, no one in the agency understands the brand as much as you do. So state your ideas with confidence that they are correct—even if you're not 100 percent sure! Second, you should be flexible. While you've done the research and you are confident, it is totally possible that you have overlooked something that is obvious to everyone else. If someone around the table asks a question about that and you realize you have missed a key point, you need to own up to it and be willing to make changes. After all, the whole point of putting the creative brief together is to have the best chance at the best advertising. And third, you should listen. Remember what we said about your research never truly being over? That is true even at the stage of the presentation of the creative brief. As you and the creative team discuss your recommendations, if you're truly listening to each person present, it is possible that you will gain a new insight during that process. If you remember to be confident and flexible and to listen, you should be able to present your brief in a true and persuasive manner. The next chapter will give you more information about making pitches.

Throughout this book, we've discussed the challenges of figuring out what advertising approach is appropriate for the brand for which you're responsible. So how does this process look from brief to finished campaign?

Let's take a look inside one agency. John Baker is the brand planning director for the Richards Group in Dallas, Texas. Someone once described John as a blue-collar guy with a white-collar mind. In other words, he is smart and business focused with an easygoing, down-home nature—a natural-born planner.

John came to the Richards Group in 1995 after 10 years in Manhattan, training in the discipline of planning at Ogilvy & Mather and DDB Needham. At the Richards Group, John has developed brand insights for a host of successful clients including Motel 6, Go RVing, and Orkin. In the past, he's worked on big clients (Campbell's Soup, Heinz, and Computer City) and small ones (Riggs Bank, Zephyrhills Bottled Water, and Antares). However, he'll be the first to say that the size of the client doesn't matter—only the size of the insight. Originally from the Syracuse area, John met his wife,

Diane, while studying at Binghamton University. He enjoys sports, reading, and his three grown kids.

Here's the creative brief for Motel 6 that John and his team developed.

THE RICHARDS GROUP CREATIVE BRIEF

People don't like advertising. People don't trust advertising. People don't remember advertising. How will we engage them?

Why are we advertising?

To convince budget-minded travelers that it's foolish to stay anywhere but Motel 6.

Whom are we talking to?

Frugal travelers who are inspired to travel. They are on their own dime and know the true value of a buck. They also know that when you close your eyes at night, all hotel rooms look alike, so they aren't willing to pay a lot for a room.

What do they currently think?

"Motel 6 is just another cheap place to stay."

What would we like them to think?

"Staying at Motel 6 is a no-brainer. It's the best deal, plain and simple. And it's not cheap, it's smart."

What is the single most persuasive idea we can convey?

At Motel 6, you get exactly what you need without paying for stuff you don't.

Why should they believe it?

Smart travelers choose Motel 6 because you get everything you really need for a comfortable night's stay at a low price. They keep things simple and strip costs so they can pass the savings on to you. And that makes Motel 6 the smart choice when all you need is sleep.

When and where is the target most receptive to our message?

When planning to spend the night away at a place that won't break the bank.

Are there any creative guidelines?

Personality: Simple, commonsensical, unpretentious, and good-humored. Include a call to action driving people to motel6.com for reservations.

CLIENT	JOB NO.
Motel 6, Inc.	
JOB TITLE	DATE
2017 TV	07/11/18

CLIENT	PLANNER	CREATIVE	BRAND MGR	MEDIA

And here is one of the radio spots that were developed from the creative brief.

CLIENT: Motel 6, Inc.
JOB: :30 RADIO
TITLE: "Designer Dogs"

> TOM: Hi, Tom Bodett. Seems it's harder than ever to find a regular ol' dog. Everybody wants some designer combination like a "Labradoodle" or "Malty-poo." And I don't even want to know what a "Schnauzeranian cockapinscher" is. But I guess if Motel 6 can combine clean, comfortable rooms with the lowest price of any national chain, you can combine anything. So you get a good night's rest, and save a shitzadoodle.
>
> I'm Tom Bodett for Motel 6, and we'll leave the light on for you. Book online at Motel6.com.

Finally, here is a short conversation with John that should help you better understand the kind of person that is attracted to account planning.

What made you want to become a planner?

The simple answer is that nothing made me want to become a planner. I got my graduate degree in the spring of 1986 and decided I would move to New York City to become an account executive at an advertising agency. It seemed like a fun career and something I might be good at, based on what I learned from going through business school and then getting my MBA. But I had a hard time getting any job in the advertising business in NYC. The economy was not great and few agencies were hiring entry-level people.

I finally met with a headhunter who mentioned that Ogilvy & Mather was starting an account planning function and was hiring people to be trained to be an account planner. I had no idea what account planning was as I'd never heard of it. But, heck, I needed a job, this was NYC, and it was at an ad agency. So, I quickly accepted, thinking I could always transfer to account management if I proved myself to be valuable enough. Fast forward a few decades and I'm still doing a lot of the same things I was first taught back in the summer of 1986.

What do you like most about planning?

I think one of the things I like are the many challenges that we face on a daily basis and figuring out how to solve those challenges. And the challenges take so many different forms from simply getting the mundane things done to solving really complex branding problems. The fact that I work on about 10 different pieces of business makes no two days ever look alike.

But what I like best is the fact that I get to help make the work better. And when I say the work, I'm mostly talking about the creative product, but I'm also referring to all aspects of the business I touch. That might include new business pitches and presentations, or it just might be an insight I have that helps the media team.

What are the characteristics of a great planner?

You would think this would be easy to answer, but it isn't. Because there are so many things that make for a great planner. Let me speak to two characteristics though. One is that great planners are talented in many different aspects of our jobs. Planning is a multidimensional discipline where we're forced to think about and do many different things. So, we're problem solvers, creative brief developers, strong writers, astute researchers, great brainstormers, keen insight developers, and creative thinkers. And we have to be bold in how we do all those things.

The second is that a great planner must also be a great storyteller. They need to be the "guy" in the room that captivates the audience and weaves an interesting brand and consumer story that has either clients, creative teams, or others in the agency leaning in. We must intrigue and we must be convincing—just like how a great story is written.

Perhaps some thoughts about insights from focus groups or in-depth interviews with consumers?

I'm not sure how to address this, but I'll try this way. No matter who I interview or whatever the category or brand is, I try to come across as not only "the moderator" but as a pseudo-friend, or better said, a confidant. This way, I can get them to open up about almost anything. I learned pretty early in my career that I could talk to just about anybody about just about anything if I played the role of a confidant. I have talked to people about really difficult and emotional topics using myself as a confidant and getting people to say things they wouldn't have expected to say to a complete stranger.

What's a fun fact or story that you like to tell about your experience as a planner?

One of the most satisfying things for me as a planner is that I get to have fun at work. Stan Richards, the sole owner of our agency, ends every meeting with the following phrase: "Let's go have fun." I've taken that to heart for the 23-plus years I've worked here. Sure, this can be a high-stress job from time to time, but as long as you keep a "let's have fun attitude," everything will be fine. And I have fun on a daily basis. It's just advertising for crying out loud. So, I don't take myself too seriously.

SUGGESTED ACTIVITIES
TO HELP YOU THINK ABOUT THIS CHAPTER

Activity 1: Choose a brand that someone in your family uses. Describe the demographics of this family member. For example, if writing about your mom, you might write, "Woman in her 50s, with a household income of about $75,000 per year." Now, expand the description to include the psychographics. For example, you might write that she is interested in reading, exercising, and traveling and pays attention to fashion.

Now write a narrative of a profile for this specific person in your target audience. While you are writing about your mom, try to step back here and describe her in a way that a stranger might view her. You might write something such as the following:

> *Jenny, now 52, is married to Johnnie, an architect who enjoys the outdoors. He often takes their golden retriever, Jesse, with him on hikes in nearby parks. Jenny is fashion conscious and interested in all the latest trends. While Johnnie is an outdoorsy type, Jenny prefers to curl up with a book when the house is quiet or get out early on a Saturday to hit different garage or yard sales. She also enjoys traveling and has been to 32 different states, and she hopes to one day check off all 50 states.*

Now, go back to your brand. Do you have any new insights that might help with developing the advertising approach? What might they be?

Activity 2: Choose a brand that you use regularly. Now take the Yakob brief (see https://farisyakob.typepad.com/files/a-new-brief-faris-yakob .pdf), and think about how you would develop the brief for your brand. Make a list of how you would go about finding the answers to each of the components in the boxes. What do you know already? What do you need to find out? How could you find this information?

Activity 3: Based on what you've read in this chapter—and the conversation with John Baker (and others throughout this book)—what appeals to you most about a job as a planner? Do you think this would be a good fit for you? Explain your thinking.

REFERENCES

Moses, S. (2018, April 10). How to write the most compelling creative brief (with examples) [Web log post]. Retrieved from https://www.workamajig.com/blog /creative-brief

Stein, L. (2018, March 29). Grey adds a question to every creative brief: How can this work reflect diversity? *Ad Age.* Retrieved from https://adage.com/article/agency -news/grey-partners-3-diversity-focused-creative/312924

Yakob, F. (2014). *Paid attention: Innovation advertising for a digital world.* London: Kogan Page Limited.

CHAPTER 14

An Account Planner's Job Is Never Done

By reading this book, we hope that you've begun to understand that account planners do and think about a lot of different things. The more experiences you can have in college, the better you can be positioned to launch your career in account planning. ReD Associates (redassociates.com), an innovative research firm, posted this statement on its webpage: "We are always looking for remarkable people. The anthropologists, sociologists, philosophers, journalists, and political scientists who make up ReD combine the methods of social and data science to study human behavior and help our clients develop perspectives on their business." That's the kind of person the forward-thinking account planner needs to be because, depending on where you work, you'll get involved in all sorts of things.

Henry Kozak, an account planner with the firm adam&eveDDB, offered a partial list of the things he does on a daily basis. These include concept testing, copy testing, writing white papers, brainstorming, pitching new business, positioning brands, segmentation studies, persona development, and customer mapping, for starters. We've discussed many of these items in previous chapters, but remember that an account planner's job is flexible. While you do many of these tasks, there are also other things you might do. However, according to Kozak the bottom line is that there are two sides to being a planner: being a problem solver and being a nurturer and idea developer.

WHITE PAPERS

Writing white papers is the kind of task you might not think of as being in the account planner's toolbox, but knowing how to write an effective white paper is a skill that will be appreciated among both your coworkers and your clients. Your client may even request that you develop a white paper for the brand. A white paper is a persuasive report that explains a problem and proposes a solution. The problem may be presented to you, but there are also times when you can be proactive and attack a potential problem that the client has yet to anticipate. If you're always thinking of your brand, staying current with trends, and thinking about your target audience—and if you're able to write your thoughts via a white paper in a persuasive manner—you'll make an important contribution to your agency.

PITCHING NEW BUSINESS

"Pitching" in its most basic form is simply making a presentation to an advertiser with the goal of convincing the brand to choose your agency as its agency of record. Agencies have all sorts of perspectives on how, why, and when to pitch new business, but it isn't unusual for the account planner to get involved in the process. Whether the agency is small or large, pitching new business is an important skill because every agency will at some time have to make a pitch. There are numerous reasons why, but here are five: (1) The agency might lose an account (or two) and need the business. (2) The agency might be ready to grow and want to pick up some new business. (3) The agency might want to keep its competitive muscles in shape. (4) The agency might want to keep its pitching skills in shape. And (5) the client makes them pitch to retain the account.

Even though the agency might be interested in improving pitching skills, the pitching process can be brutal and expensive, so it isn't something entered into lightly. Typically, an advertising agency wants to hold on to a client once it has the client, but this isn't always possible (another reason for the agency to be "pitch ready"). Sometimes, the advertiser decides that it will look for a new agency—or that it wants its agency to have to prove again that the agency of record knows how best to represent the brand. Or they may have decided they need to change strategies, and they want to see if their agency can support that approach. Or the client might decide it needs to cut costs and will ask its agency of record to pitch under the new budget model.

Because it's so expensive (both in time and money), usually just a handful of agencies will pitch for new business with the same client. For example, when Airbnb decided to part ways with TBWA/Chiat/Day LA, only two agencies pitched: Wieden + Kennedy and DDB. (Wieden + Kennedy won the account.)

When an advertiser makes a major marketing strategy change, it's not unusual that the advertising agency has to change as well. At the end of 2017, for example, McDonald's decided to conduct its first global agency review in 10 years. They required its longtime agency OMD to repitch the account. McDonald's wanted to move from a single-agency model to a "small roster" agency. So even if OMD won the pitch, it would be losing out on some significant billings.

Recently, some agencies have started to fight back a bit on the "agency pitching world." Droga5 is one such agency. They bill themselves as "Creatively Led. Strategically Driven. Digitally Native. Humanity Obsessed." The principals at Droga5 argue that agencies should only pitch new business if they are at least 50% sure they can win the business. And interestingly, they also argue that an agency should only pitch if they will be paid for the work they present.

The pitching process can be different for different advertisers. Even so, the common components of a pitch are as follows: (1) A request for proposal (RFP) giving the parameters of what the advertiser is looking for, deadlines for the work, and other information that the advertiser deems important. (2) Initial meeting. This is usually a two-way "look see" for both the advertiser and the agency to get a sense if this relationship will be a good one. (3) Sharing "rough ideas." Again, this is still a two-way approach. The advertiser can see if the agency "gets them," and the agency can see if the advertiser can tune in to how the agency might want to approach the brand.

If both the advertiser and the agency make it through these first three steps together, then it will be time for the final push and the formal presentation. During the final presentation (the actual pitch), ideas that are presented are critical, but how they are presented is just as important. As an advertising student, it may be years before you have to worry about pitching new business in an agency, but "giving it a try" now as a student can help you gain insights into your future career.

As we discussed earlier, as an account planner you may need to give a formal pitch to the creatives about the creative brief you have created. Also, if you participate in any student advertising competitions such as the AAF's National Student Advertising Competition, you'll need to develop your pitching skills. So, here are some pointers to get you started: (1) Make sure your materials are as strong as you can make them (and fit into the parameters of the requirements). (2) Speak clearly and with confidence. (3) Keep your presentation to the required time frame. (4) During the question-and-answer period, listen carefully to the questions and answer honestly. And (5) believe you can win this competition, but be gracious if you don't.

Advertising agencies aren't the only companies rethinking the pitching process. Some advertisers also have begun to rethink how they ask agencies to pitch for new business. For example, Michael Fanuele, former chief creative officer of General Mills, had this to say about pitching: "It's brutal. The time demanded, on top of the pressure exerted, on top of the very real jobs at risk—especially in the case of a large and complex multi-brand assignment—is literally life-altering for those participating" (Fanuele, 2017). So, General Mills developed a different approach to how they wanted to see agencies pitch. First, they set up an initial meeting for an informal conversation as each entity learns about the other. Second, they let the agency meet with all sorts of key personnel of the company to have honest conversations about what they hope to do, anticipated struggles, and other issues they might anticipate. General Mills then leaves the potential advertising agency with one "searing" question for the agency to ponder for a few weeks. Finally, they have a "creative conversation" as they hear from the agency on how it thinks it can answer that question.

When it comes to pitching business, it's extremely important to understand that there are seismic shifts happening not only at communication companies but also at the advertisers. You learned about Procter & Gamble in chapter 4 under "Brand Architecture." As you now know, P&G is one of the iconic companies that exemplifies the "House of Brands" approach. In late 2017, P&G decided to reduce its number of agencies. Jon Moeller, CFO, said that P&G would be reducing its number of agencies from 6,000 to 2,500. While this represents a tremendous reorganization, obviously P&G still requires a large number of agencies because of its numerous brands. Moeller, in this announcement, said P&G would be focusing on both improving the message and developing consumer insights. If you haven't seen the importance of account planning before now, that comment from such a powerful executive at such an expansive and advertising-heavy corporation should change your mind.

Advertising continues to reinvent itself and will continue to do so in the future. That's why we believe the role of account planning will only continue to become more important as agencies evolve.

Remember the checklist to see if you had the qualities of a good account planner that we started with in chapter 1? Let's go back and take a look.

1. *Curiosity.* After reading this book, you should realize that the account planner's job takes creativity. Whether it's creating personas, engaging in mind mapping, or writing an advertising strategy, those who can think creatively will succeed at a level that others can't.
2. *Media appreciation.* When you read chapter 7 on "Social Media Monitoring Tools," were you excited and ready to get started? Do you look at your Facebook newsfeed in a different way now? Are you less likely to "skip the ad in 4 seconds" when watching a YouTube video?
3. *Creative research skills.* We hope that after reading the chapters on research, you have come to realize that this is "research with personality." You can't just report the numbers. You need to figure out a pithy way to explain what the numbers mean.

4. *Making connections.* You should also have realized after reading the book that the account planner makes connections all the time. Whether it's the brand and the consumer, the consumer and the latest trend, or the problem and the solution, being able to make connections is key to becoming a successful account planner.

5. *Reading voraciously.* The fact that you've made it this far in the book is a good sign that you're a reader. But remember—don't stop with "required" reading. The astute account planners understand that they need to keep their brain sharp and always be thinking of and looking for that next great insight.

6. *Enthusiastic writer.* Even though the account planner's job can vary from agency to agency, one skill is always required: the ability to write well. So start now. Write often, whether it's required or not. Develop your enthusiasm for writing, and you'll improve your chances at succeeding as an account planner.

7. *Neuroscience appreciation.* As a voracious reader, you'll come across all sorts of new discoveries in the realm of neuroscience. Pay attention. The more you understand how the brain works, the better prepared you'll be for a career in account planning.

Rob Sellars, a strategist with AMV BBDO, has said that being an account planner is like being a detective. Throughout this book, we've tried to explain the process of account planning by demonstrating the many different aspects of the job. But at the heart of the planner is one of "wanting to solve a problem." Just like Sellars has said, account planners are detectives. That means you have to work hard, think about things differently, and connect information together in a way that leads you to a creative solution.

The legendary cellist Yo-Yo Ma has reportedly said, "Passion is one great force that unleashes creativity because if you're passionate about something, you're more willing to take risks." After reading this book, we hope that you might become passionate about advertising in general and account planning in particular. If you have the desire, you can do it.

As you finish reading *Advertising Account Planning: New Strategies in the Digital Landscape,* let's end by hearing from one more account planner.

Kendra Salvatore is the head of strategy at BBH New York where she has worked for seven years. While at BBH she has worked on a range of clients such as Google, PlayStation, Cole Haan, Grubhub, and Brighthouse Financial. In addition, she is the founder of BBH for Good, a consultancy that uses strategy and creativity to drive success for brands and social issues. At BBH, she has also held strategist and strategy director roles. Prior to BBH, Kendra was a senior strategist at Now What Research, a qualitative research and strategy firm, for clients including ESPN, Nestlé, Coca-Cola, and NBC. Before that, she was a brand strategist at Kirshenbaum Bond Senecal + Partners (recently renamed Forsman & Bodenfors) working on Wendy's and Starz entertainment. Over her career Kendra's strategic work has been recognized at the Effie Awards, the Jay Chiat Awards, the IAB awards, and the Cannes Creative Effectiveness Awards. Kendra went to New York University's Gallatin School of Individualized Study, where she created her own major called the "psychology of design" and practiced oil painting.

Is your degree in psychology of design? Is that degree in the design or the psychology department? What was the focus?

My degree is in the psychology of design from the Gallatin School of Individualized Study at NYU. At Gallatin, each student creates their own major and is supported with specialized curriculum and faculty across relevant subject matter.

The psychology of design explored the relationship between aesthetics and human needs and how they influence each other. The priority academic subjects included media, politics, psychology, and art; I studied art and oil painting.

What made you want to become a planner?

As an artist, I placed a lot of importance on coming up with what the idea should be about, looking at who had communicated this idea before and thinking about how my new work would need to be crafted to cause people to feel or act differently.

When I found out there was a discipline in advertising that helped creative teams in this way, it was a perfect match. I didn't want to be a creative because digital creativity wasn't the same satisfaction to me personally as painting on a canvas.

I also wanted to become a planner because in advertising we measure creativity and we get to know if people actually felt or did the things we intended, and we learn from that. Other forms of creativity don't necessarily have as good of a human feedback loop, and that is important to me in order to be a great creative communicator.

What do you like most about planning?

Planning is the first frontier of creativity. We have the responsibility to make sure we're creating the best possible starting point for creative work that will eventually be seen by lots of human beings—and throughout the process we make sure that work is the best creative expression it can be, so it's actually good for people and the businesses we help. I like this because I think a lot of advertising isn't good, but people are still forced to watch it. Planners should make sure our ideas and work is valued and not blocked, cut, or criticized.

What are the characteristics of a great planner?

They don't just accept things as they are, they care about finding the best possible idea or outcome, [and] they are restless.

Their ideas are equal parts "intelligence and magic," a lightning strike that can ignite business, human behavior, and creativity.

They are collaborative, open minded, and positive. Advertising at its best is a team of smart, creative people who make better work when they work together. It's not about being right or precious—and that's not as fun anyway!

What are your thoughts about insights from focus groups or in-depth interviews with consumers?

Claude Lévi-Strauss said, "The wise man is not he who gives the right answers; he is the one who asks the right questions." Any research is an opportunity to understand people we normally don't get to talk to about their values in life. This is one of the great privileges of being a planner.

No matter the methodology, it's our responsibility to ask the right questions that are thoughtful, caring, and get to the heart of how what we do can improve their lives in big or small ways.

What's your favorite way of finding the consumer insight?

Journals. People tell you incredible and original things when they have private time to think and write. Then, use the richness you find as stimulus to continue your research and scale it through quantitative tools.

What's a fun fact or story that you'd like to tell about your experience as a planner?

In my first planning job I worked on Wendy's. We did a lot of R&D focus groups for cheeseburgers. My boss was a vegan, and the other strategist was a vegetarian, so when the clients would bring back the product to taste, I had to eat all the cheeseburgers myself.

SUGGESTED ACTIVITIES
TO HELP YOU THINK ABOUT THIS CHAPTER

Activity 1: Would you like to be part of an agency's pitch team? Discuss the various aspects of a pitch and what role you would like to play. Would you enjoy this? Do you think you'd be good at this? Do you like the idea of always pitching new business but not working on an actual account if the agency wins the business?

Activity 2: Look again at the seven-item checklist with the qualities of a good planner in this chapter. Go through each one and say, "Yep, that's something I do." Or, "Nope, that's not who I am." Of the seven, how many did you say yes to? If you checked off most of these, you might find a home as a planner.

Activity 3: Look at Kendra Salvatore's list of "What are the characteristics of a great planner?" How many of these do you think are part of who you are? Do you think you might be a good planner? Why or why not?

REFERENCES

Fanuele, M. (2017, February 24). An open letter to clients considering an ad agency review: Part 2. *Ad Age*. Retrieved from https://adage.com/article/viewpoint/open-letter-clients-ad-agency-review-part-2/308050

Index